2004

ON(A RHYME

IMAGINATION FOR
A NEW GENERATION

Poems From
Devon & Cornwall
Edited by Sarah Marshall

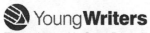 Young**Writers**

First published in Great Britain in 2005 by:
Young Writers
Remus House
Coltsfoot Drive
Peterborough
PE2 9JX
Telephone: 01733 890066
Website: www.youngwriters.co.uk

SB ISBN 1 84460 668 6

Foreword

Young Writers was established in 1991 and has been passionately devoted to the promotion of reading and writing in children and young adults ever since. The quest continues today. Young Writers remains as committed to engendering the fostering of burgeoning poetic and literary talent as ever.

This year's Young Writers competition has proven as vibrant and dynamic as ever and we are delighted to present a showcase of the best poetry from across the UK. Each poem has been carefully selected from a wealth of *Once Upon A Rhyme* entries before ultimately being published in this, our twelfth primary school poetry series.

Once again, we have been supremely impressed by the overall high quality of the entries we have received. The imagination, energy and creativity which has gone into each young writer's entry made choosing the best poems a challenging and often difficult but ultimately hugely rewarding task - the general high standard of the work submitted amply vindicating this opportunity to bring their poetry to a larger appreciative audience.

We sincerely hope you are pleased with our final selection and that you will enjoy *Once Upon A Rhyme Poems From Devon & Cornwall* for many years to come.

Contents

Billie Knowles (9)   16

Bickleigh-On-Exe Primary School, Tiverton
Jake Dascombe (9)   16
Connie Yeoman (10)   16
Kimberley Meech (10)   17
Kathryn Letheren (9)   17
Sarah Weber (10)   18
Luke Chanin (10)   18
Ben Colston (9)   18
Tanith Gould (9)   19
Alex Parslow (10)   19
James Collard (10)   19
Alexandra Dudley (9)   20
Charlotte Alsopp (9)   20
Andrew Bennett (10)   20
Lorna Callahan (10)   21
Robbie Williams (10)   21
Adam Farr (11)   21
Lauren Wiggins (10)   22
Peter Wright (10)   22
Kyrin Wiggins (10)   22
Chantelle Reid (10)   23
Cathryn Buechel (10)   23
Rhys Faram (10)   23
Emma Hird (10)   24
Tom Huxtable (10)   24
Eddie Knowles (10)   24

Bishops Tawton CP School, Barnstaple
John Leaver (9)   25

Bradley Rowe Middle School, Exeter
Emily Brice (8)   26
Lauren Jenkins (8)   26
Samantha Burnham (8)   27
Sinead Cummings (8)   27
Ellie-Mae Bamford (8)   28
Oliver Moore (8)   28
Danielle Framingham (8)   29
Ryan Challice (8)   29

Joshua Jones (8)	30
Dan Gallagher (8)	30
Tommy Morgan (8)	31
Keiran Brown (8)	31
Shannon Hutchings (8)	32
John Lindsay (9)	32
Jodie Vinicombe (8)	33
Charlotte Selley (8)	33
Adam Reed (8)	34
Shannon Cole (8)	34
Lauren Woodcock (8)	35
Emily Cleave (8)	35
Paula Hill (8)	36
Sophie Ball (8)	36
Ryan Harding (8)	37
Chloe Reed (8)	37
Jaid Spinks (8)	38
Laura Rogers (8)	38
Stephanie Lambshead (8)	39
Aron Hutchings (8)	39
Lauren Evans (9)	40
Katie Mundell (8)	40

Bratton Fleming Primary School, Barnstaple

Mary Elsie Hawkins (10)	41
Silas Clay (9)	41
Florence Cotten (10)	42
Luke Thorne (9)	42
Vashti Cotten (9)	43
Sara Beth Ling (10)	43
Jack Mullen (9)	44
Sophie Land (10)	44
Lydia Huxtable (9)	45
Lily Northam (9)	45
Holly Ling (10)	46
Tim Huxtable (10)	46
Matthew Essery (10)	47
Natalie Clarke (9)	47
James Thomas (10)	48
Charlie Rooke (10)	48
Johnathan Shapland (9)	49

Brayford CP School, Barnstaple

Reuben Greenidge (10)	49
Helen Thomas (10)	50
Ben Thorne (9)	50
Pippa Byrne (9)	51
Sam Wildig (9)	51
Freddie Jones (9)	52
Chilli Small (8)	52
Willow Beauchamp (8)	52
Terri-Anne Groves (9)	53
William Osborne (7)	53
Gemma Heal (10)	53
Bethany Pearson (9)	54
Aaron Beauchamp (7)	54
Ben Jones (7)	55
Sarah Thomas (7)	55
Connie Heal (7)	56
Sean Dallyn (10)	56
Oliver Maundrell (10)	57
Jessica Furlong (7)	57

Canada Hill CP School, Newton Abbot

Natasha Murch (10)	58
Jacob Scotte-Hatherly (9)	58
James Brookman (10)	59
Kamisha Adams (9)	59
Jack Wotton (9)	60
Daniel Henderson (9)	61
Lois Gill (9)	62
Sophie Hyslop (10)	62
Jack Lewis (10)	63
Megan Kingsley-Smith (11)	63
Fay Sawkins (9)	64
Luke Nicholls (10)	64
Rachael Guilfoyle (10)	65
James McGladdery (10)	65
Shannon Pitts (9)	66
Louise Hawkyard (10)	67
Ryan Rogers (9)	68
Matthew Fox (10)	68
Thomas Sellick (10)	69

Glenn Stephens (11)	69
Sam Kelly (10)	70
Laura Nott (10)	70
Ryan Partridge (10)	71
Hayley Gilbert (10)	71
Ben Fawcett (10)	72
Luke Keaveney (10)	73
Thomas Glover (9)	74
Imogen Uniacke (9)	74
Edward Glanville (11)	74
Katie Mill-Gammin (9)	75
Kandi Noble (10)	75
Katie Gale (9)	75
George Burton (9)	76
Jordan Simpson (9)	76
Lily Luscombe (10)	76
Abigail Hewings (10)	77
Chloe Brown (10)	77
Gabriel Bailey (9)	77
Aimee Myers (10)	78
Ben Ames (10)	79
Emma Houdmont (11)	79
Joseph Richards (10)	80
Beth Norrish (9)	80
Heather Buttifant (9)	81
Josh Castree (10)	81
Rachel Fogden (11)	82
Samuel Wakeham (11)	82
Lily Smith (10)	83
Ashleigh Dummett (10)	83
Rachel Craig	84
Natasha Knott (9)	84
Tarquin Warren (9)	85
Oliver Hensberg (10)	85
Jessica Powell (10)	86
Matthew Frankpitt (9)	86
Josie Roberts (10)	86
Kate Baverstock-White (10)	87
Stephen Powell (9)	87
Corin Yabsley (10)	88
Jade Steventon (9)	88
Connor Mantle (9)	88

Brittany Caple (10)	89
Bryony Larkin (9)	89
James Cluer (9)	90
Zoe Paddon (11)	91
Matthew Cole (10)	92
Ben Roughley (10)	92
Daniel Webber (9)	93
Jennifer Robinson (10)	93
George Morris (10)	94
Liam Price (9)	94
Richard Maddison (10)	95

Carclaze Junior School, St Austell
Abigail Maude (10)	95

Crowan Primary School, Camborne
Mark Delaney (10)	96
Christopher Vincent (10)	96
Jake Janes (10)	96
Oliver Hickey (10)	97
Tom James (9)	97
Annabel Hawken (10)	97
Becki Kennelly (11)	98
Joshua Thomas (10)	98
Lily Edwards (10)	98
Kieran Woolcock (10)	99
Shannen Barton (10)	99
Paul Fisher (10)	100
Liana Goss (9)	100
David Hilliard (10)	100
Harry Edwards (8)	101
Billy Reid (10)	101
William Henderson (8)	101
Emma Winder (10)	102
Emily Masterton (10)	102
Rhys Fairlie (8)	103
Oliver McGeorge (9)	103

Ellacombe CP School, Torquay
Jennifer Booth (10)	103
Abigail Bratcher (10)	104

Lympstone CE Primary School, Lympstone

Siobhan Riggs (10)	117
Rebecca Brown (10)	117
Jasmine Ousley (10)	118
Georgia Goff (10)	118
Michael Lockhart (10)	118
Kelsey Clayton (11)	119
Jack Gardner (10)	119
Carla Griffin (10)	119
Lauren Mingo (10)	120
Behn Wright (10)	120
Sophie Morgan (10)	120
Jack Amphlett (10)	121

Marhamchurch Primary School, Bude

Gabby Reynolds & Clovie Knight (10)	121
Louise Kerr (10)	122

Moretonhampstead Primary School, Newton Abbot

Anna Newman (9)	122
Sarah Stewart-Watson (9)	123
Caroline Francis (10)	123
Sam Goodwyn (10)	124
Lorine Parkinson (10)	124
Hollie Brackenbury (10)	125
Rebekah Austin (9)	125
Tommy Newell (9)	125
Joe Colridge (9)	126
Hannah Austin (9)	126
Cara Bell (10)	126
Hannah Goodwin (9)	127
Teresa Hellyer (9)	127
Lisa Tribe (10)	128
Kimberley Thomas (10)	128
Alex Amery (10)	129
Scarlett Garland (10)	129
Charlotte Farrer (10)	130
Harry Hampton (10)	130

St Mellion CE Primary School, Saltash

Iesha Chaney (8)	131
Holly Hemmens (8)	131
Luke Hewison (8)	132
Ben Jeffery (7)	132
Joseph Grocott (8)	133
Dominick Chiswell (8)	133
Rhianna Darby (9)	134
Amelia Fox (9)	134
Sophie Northcott (9)	135
Christopher Dwane (9)	135
Dean Lambert (9)	136
Liam Maton (9)	136
Ben Farrar (11)	137
Dan Ball (10)	137
Alex Jeffery (9)	138
Tim Page (10)	138
Joshua Paul (10)	139
Tom Ransome (10)	139

Sampford Peverell CE Primary School, Tiverton

Alex Everett (10)	140
Margaret Palmer (9)	140

Tregony Primary School, Tregony

Samuel Kendall (8)	141
Zoe Waters (8)	142
Lauren Shearing (9)	142
Conor Pearce (8)	143
Georgie Green (7)	143
Chris Thomas (9)	143
Brannon Cummins (8)	144
Chloe Ringrose (9)	144
Robert Wilshaw (8)	145
Elowen Gray-Roberts (7)	145
Amanda Butfield (9)	145
Curtis Cowl (8)	146
Sophie Jackson (8)	146
Jacob Bunney (7)	146
Eleanor Wood (8)	147
Nichola Goldworthy (8)	147

Ysabelle Smith (7)	147
Sean Gibson (8)	148
Jack Emery (8)	148
Nathan Cowl (9)	148
Rachael O'Brien (8)	149
Andrew Barton (7)	149
Michael Berridge (8)	149
Bethany Grant (7)	150
Thomas Oatey (7)	150
Elizabeth Oatey (8)	150

Troon Primary School, Camborne

Claire Thompson (10)	151
Amber Wise (10)	151
Amber Mankee (10)	152
Liam Kevern (11)	152
Paige Bennett (10)	153
Yasmin Baker (10)	153
Liam Spear (10)	154
Bradley Mills (10)	154
Daniel Buckingham (10)	155
Ebony Ellis (10)	155
Zack Cooper (10)	156
Bethany Gould (11)	156
Aimee Mayhew Brokenshire (10)	156
Amy Andrew (10)	157
David Wills (10)	157
Madeleine Moore (10)	158
Caine Hocking (10)	158

Two Moors Primary School, Tiverton

Lauren Saunders (8)	159
Harriot Taylor (8)	159
Caitlin Owen (8)	159
Mikesh Mistry (8)	160
Megan Buckingham (8)	160
Cody Norwell (9)	160
Emily Payne (8)	161
Kieron Chard-Maple (8)	161
Jessica Willis (9)	161
Jake Ware (8)	162

Louise Jessett (7)	179
Sam Eyres (7)	180
Laura Hesketh (8)	180
Isobel Fern (7)	180
Eleanor Crimmen (8)	181
Abigail Beswick Lund (7)	181
Jonathan Pascoe (9)	181
Jake Robertson (8)	182
Jessica Goodchild (7)	182
Rachael Thomas (8)	182
Claudia Corbridge (8)	183
Jade Wooderson Harrod (9)	183
Eloise Thwaites (8)	184
Joseph Martin (7)	184
Nicholas Phillips (7)	185
Amber Wooderson Harrod (7)	185
Emily Rhodes (7)	185
William Jose (7)	186
Niamh Cook (8)	186
Lowena Mudge (7)	186
Alice Harry (8)	187
Gabrielle Slater (7)	187
Heather MacNeil (7)	188

Widewell Primary School, Plymouth

Holly Hobbs (10)	188
Dylan Gowlett (9)	189
George Harding (9)	189
Loren Smith (9)	189
Katie Fallick (11)	190
Frances Bennison-Reseigh (10)	190
Andrew Hunter (10)	191
Shannon Limbrick (10)	191
Connor Palfreeman (10)	192

Withycombe Raleigh CE School, Exmouth

Max Lewin (9)	192
Ben Mellish (9)	193
Max Williams (9)	194
Jack Greenhalgh (9)	194
Chris Rundle (9)	195

The Poems

When I Am Happy I . . .

When I am happy I
Zoom down the hill on my scooter.

When I am happy I
Pick blackberries at the fort.

When I am happy I
Help Mummy bake my favourite cake.

When I am happy I
Watch Dick and Dom in the bungalow.

When I am happy I
Read my joke book.

Poppy Flaxman (8)
Appledore Primary School, Bideford

When I Am Happy I . . .

When I am happy I
Play badminton with my friends.

When I am happy I
Watch Cartoon Network on my TV.

When I am happy I
Play on my Game Cube.

When I am happy my
Heart beats wildly.

When I am happy I
Practise football in the park.

Christian Tucker (8)
Appledore Primary School, Bideford

When I Am Happy I . . .

When I am happy I
Take my fluffy dog for long breezy strolls on the sandy beach.

When I am happy I
Give my mum and dad hugs.

When I am happy I
Make my mum and dad nice things.

When I am happy I
Smile at everyone.

When I am happy I
Go shopping with my sister.

Amber Smith (8)
Appledore Primary School, Bideford

When I Am Happy I . . .

When I am happy I
Go out shopping with my fabulous friends.

When I am happy I
Go and visit my friend.

When I am happy I
Go to Plymouth swimming pool.

When I am happy I
Go to my cousin's house.

When I am happy I
Go and shop in Barnstaple.

Lauren Haydock (8)
Appledore Primary School, Bideford

When I Am Happy I . . .

When I am happy I
Do tricks with my best mates.

When I am happy I
Have a big smile

When I am happy I
Go outside and play cricket.

When I am happy I
Cheer.

When I am happy I
Am funny.

Joshua Atkinson (8)
Appledore Primary School, Bideford

When I Am Happy I . . .

When I am happy I
Like to smile, joke and laugh.

When I am happy I
Play with my nice friends.

When I am happy I
Like to skip all day.

When I am happy I
Play on the climbing frame.

When I am happy I
Play with my good dog.

Jennifer McCann (8)
Appledore Primary School, Bideford

When I Am Happy I . . .

When I am happy I
Skip over to my friend's house.

When I am happy I
Have a big smile on my face.

When I am happy I
Go outside and do cartwheels.

When I am happy I
Go and buy sweets.

When I am happy I
Ride my shiny pink bike.

Emily Marler (8)
Appledore Primary School, Bideford

When I Am Happy I . . .

When I am happy I
Play on my Xbox.

When I am happy I
Play with my mates.

When I am happy I
Play on my bike.

Brandon Hughes (8)
Appledore Primary School, Bideford

When I Am Happy I . . .

When I am happy I
Play a game of football.

When I am happy I
Go swimming in the swimming pool.

Jack Sharrock (8)
Appledore Primary School, Bideford

When I Am Happy I . . .

When I am happy I
Go for a fast ride on my purple bike.

When I am happy I
Go body-boarding in the sea.

When I am happy I
Hear the trees sway gracefully in the breeze.

When I am happy I
Have a smile on my face.

Daisy Lavington (8)
Appledore Primary School, Bideford

When I Am Happy I . . .

When I am happy I
Play on my PS2 for five minutes.

When I am happy I
Ride my BMX in the park with my dad.

When I am happy I
Watch TV whenever I want too.

When I am happy I
Play football in my garden and the park.

Joshua Stephenson (8)
Appledore Primary School, Bideford

When I Am Happy I . . .

When I am happy I
Play in the sandpit.

When I am happy I
Talk with my chipmunk.

When I am happy I
Like to go swimming.

Macgowan Blundell (8)
Appledore Primary School, Bideford

When I Am Happy I . . .

When I am happy I
Am jolly.

When I am happy I
Smile in laughter.

When I am happy I
Ride my pink bike that shines in the dark.

When I am happy I
Go swimming in the blue sea.

When I am happy I
Go fishing in the still water.

When I am happy I
Go down to the icy cold beach.

Rosie Cole (9)
Appledore Primary School, Bideford

Anger

Anger stares at me like an evil demon from Hell
Dancing around a blazing fire.
It's as gigantic as an enormous fire-breathing dragon
Stomping fiercely in my brain
So supersonic fast it's impossible to see.
As loud as a deafening volcano exploding in my head,
Its taste makes me sick like an oozing slimy,
Slithering slug slipping up my tongue.
The smell is so revolting.
It smells like a bin full of rotten fish
And old babies' nappies that follow me around.
I'm on my knees begging for it to go away.
But it said, 'No, I'm here to stay!'

Shannon Cox (9)
Appledore Primary School, Bideford

Anger

It howls in my battered bunk bed,
As the outraging orange breath mouth.
It makes a disgusting air-freshener in my room,
Dribbles all over my carpet,
It stomps all over my T-shirts and socks,
Its sparkly ice covered hair, makes it impossible to see its fierce,
                                        fiery eyes,
It stomps on me like ten thousand animals trampling and tripping
                                        over my legs.
But every blink I take it seems to get bigger . . . and bigger . . .
                                        and bigger.
I feel frozen,
I hope it's just a dream.

Katie-Ellen Boyes (9)
Appledore Primary School, Bideford

Anger

It starts as small as a crumb,
When you hardly notice it's there,
He grows every time I get angry to the size of a charging rhino.
He speeds off up to my room,
He is faster than a cheetah.
The smell of rotting rubbish runs around my room.
Its glowing green and red flare freezes me on the spot.
The voice of a demon is what I can hear, like nails on a chalkboard,
Again and again and again,
At night he sits at the end of my bed,
The air is as cold as a frozen bath,
I ask, 'Can you please go away?' but he says
'I am here to *stay!*'

Brandon Rockey (9)
Appledore Primary School, Bideford

When I Am Happy I . . .

When I am happy my
Brain tells my legs to jump around.

When I am happy I
Play on my sister's PlayStation.

When I am happy I
Play Cluedo against my unbeatable sister.

When I am happy I
Dive in the blue swimming pool.

Georgina Jury (8)
Appledore Primary School, Bideford

Anger

Anger's touch is as hot as boiling lava,
And creeps like a spinning, slippery spider crawling over me.
It tastes like a mouldy apple.
It stinks like rotten cheese.
It groans like a devil.
It grows like a balloon.
It glares at me with glowing red and green eyes.
It vanishes like a ghost.
I'm glad.

Deron Jones (9)
Appledore Primary School, Bideford

Anger

Anger smells like slippery, sour cream,
Anger tastes like rotten bananas,
Anger moves like a sleek, sly cat ready to catch a beautiful bird.
Anger sounds like the nails of a witch that screech down a blackboard.
When I tell it to go away it won't.
It frightens me.

Ellenor Phillips (9)
Appledore Primary School, Bideford

Anger

Anger looks at me with a glare like crinkly, crunched up
                                        crisp packets,
Anger tastes like a slippery sour lemon on my tingling taste buds,
Anger is like a scaly snake, slithering across my hairy legs,
Anger starts off the size of a crumb, gets to the size of a giant
And then it explodes like darting dynamite.
Anger reeks like stale socks in a revolting rubbish heap.
Anger's speech is like my mum shouting loudly at me
When I make her madly stressed.
My mum says it will go away when I sleep tonight
And it will not be there when I wake up.
That's what my mum says but I think she is making it up.

Lucy Powe (9)
Appledore Primary School, Bideford

Anger

Anger started as small as an apple pie then,
Grows like fiery flames on a bonfire,
Anger is as rotten as a piece of old blue cheese,
He follows me,
Anger is slow and moody, he growls and barks like a dog,
He's as spicy as a chilli in a Mexican way,
He has red, enormous, fiery flames for eyes,
A touch will send shivers down my spine,
He's slimy but cold like a snail on a winter's day.

Saxon Bowden (9)
Appledore Primary School, Bideford

Anger

Anger stares at me like a scary story,
Anger screams at me like bursting blisters,
Anger's smell is a reek that makes me frighteningly sick,
Anger moves towards me like ball lightning.

Luke Hasted (9)
Appledore Primary School, Bideford

Anger

Anger stares at me like a massive lion waiting to pounce.
All over it's bumpy and lumpy like a crocodile's back.
It smells like a bit of old, rotten, blue cheese.
It speaks so fast that I can't hear it properly.
It tastes like sour, stinging lemon.
It slithers slowly, slyly across my bedroom floor.
It grows like a tarantula, a Komodo dragon to a man-eating tiger.
Mum says it's fake, I say it's real.
But there's really no telling.

Rebecca Hadden (9)
Appledore Primary School, Bideford

Anger

Anger has flaming eyes,
Like burning lasers.
It reeks like old bones and dead rats.
It slithers like a snake sliding on me.
It speaks to me like a blown up building.
Its touch is like a kidnapper's gunshot,
I hate anger, it never goes away.

Jaz Rogers (9)
Appledore Primary School, Bideford

Anger

Anger is a gigantic fiery bear,
Anger smells like some rotten, gone off cheese.
It tastes of rotten eggs.
It moves like vampires in the blazing hot desert.
Anger glares at me with its long blazing eyes.
Anger touches me with a big hard thump.
It growls aggressively like an enormous hungry bear.
But now anger is gone, it flew away and I never saw it again.

Amy Fisher (10)
Appledore Primary School, Bideford

Anger

Anger is a monster,
A monster that has eyes like fiery flames
Which strike at me with lightning speed.
Its smell is like revolting cheese.
I feel like running away
But it will follow.
Its claws with razor-sharp blades sprint after me
Like cat paws.
There are gigantic teeth pointing out of its jaws.
Anger is here to stay.

Jesse Curtis (10)
Appledore Primary School, Bideford

Anger

Anger tastes disgusting, spit it out.
It smells like you want to be sick,
Anger's eyes burn like lasers.
It speaks loud and scary and
Moves like thunder and lightning.
Anger is large, it's enormous.
The touch of anger makes your heart pump fast.

Harry Monks (9)
Appledore Primary School, Bideford

Anger

Anger watches as I stagger across the pathway.
I try to run but it always catches up.
Anger brushes me like a blazing, burning brush,
Anger barks like a wolf fiercely,
Anger reeks like muddy pigs rolling in mud.
Anger is as clever as an old owl,
Anger suddenly vanishes into thin air.

James Greenleaf (9)
Appledore Primary School, Bideford

Anger

Anger is like a huge elephant stomping towards me,
Anger watches me like a slithering squashed snake,
Which scares me.
Anger mutters at me repeating,
'Do it! Do it!'
Anger's touch is like a stroke.
Anger's smell is like burning flesh,
Which disgusts me.
I shout, 'Go away! Go away!'

Ben Shapland (9)
Appledore Primary School, Bideford

Anger

Anger has come to stay, it won't go away,
But it doesn't listen to me.
Anger stares with gloomy, red eyes,
Anger screams to annoy me.
Anger is ready to pounce like a puma
Which jumps on its prey.
Anger's smell is like really smelly socks,
Anger's touch is like a slice through my hands,
Anger is always ready to jump.

Michelle Stanley (9)
Appledore Primary School, Bideford

Anger

Anger dresses like a vampire,
Anger smells like rotten rats,
Anger speaks to me like a head teacher,
It won't go away.
Anger moves like a sprinter in the Olympics.
Anger stares at me with evil eyes,
Anger stabs me like a kidnapper.

Brogan Foster (9)
Appledore Primary School, Bideford

Anger

Anger's four square eyes glow and follow me now and then.
Anger speaks weirdly and walks from side to side.
Anger is as small and as big as a tarantula.
Anger reeks like rotten, blue, three-month-old cheese.
Anger's taste is a sour curry
Spicy on my drastic, tingling, tickedly tangled hairy legs.
When anger is touched
It feels like a sweet furry fur.
It shivers like its ice cubes in an ice-cold lake.

Natalie Michael (9)
Appledore Primary School, Bideford

Anger

Anger glares at me like an alien ready to shoot,
Anger's smell is like a mouldy pizza,
Anger creeps dangerously,
Anger's stab is like a lion pouncing on me,
Anger is a roaring bomb blowing up,
Like an elephant sitting on top of me.
Finally the anger has disappeared,
I hope it doesn't come back.

Thomas Atkinson (9)
Appledore Primary School, Bideford

Anger

Anger came to stay in my room,
I glance at him, he glances back.
His breath smells like raw sick,
He tastes like a smelly sock.
Anger moves around the walls,
Anger speaks and spits.
He touches me as if I've known him for years.

Ryan Bale-Grant (9)
Appledore Primary School, Bideford

Anger

Anger's speech is an evil devil,
It started off as a little crumb and grows
Until it's the size of an elephant.
Every day I wake up I always smell that funny smell
Like out of date milk.
With his huge glary eyes, always ready to start its power.
I am so scared.
Every time it comes to me I start to get hotter and hotter,
I begin to sweat.
It tastes of chilli pepper.
I want it to go away so I ask
'Can you find someone else?'
'No,' it says, 'I am here to stay.'

Cerri Gaskin (9)
Appledore Primary School, Bideford

Anger

Anger smells like really old pongy socks,
Anger's eyes are as wide as a window,
Anger is different sizes from a rat to a pig
And then a kangaroo to an elephant.
Anger sounds like fingernails being run down a chalkboard.
Anger tastes like eating a magnet.
Anger creeps up on me when I least expect it and pounces on me,
So I am really scared.
And then it fades away, slower and slower and slower until
It's gone.

Danielle Bond (9)
Appledore Primary School, Bideford

Anger

Anger's eyes are like a strong magnet attached to another,
They look like fire flaming beams.
He smells like burning skin.
He follows me.
He mumbles slowing and repeats over and over again
'Get angry! Get angry! Get angry!'
He grows like a fast growing cub that never stops.
His taste is like you have just been to the dentist
And had some numbness put on your gums.
His touch is like you have just stapled your thumb.
I tell him at night to go away,
But he still comes back the next day.

Sam Hudson (9)
Appledore Primary School, Bideford

Anger

Anger screeches fiercely at me,
Anger's demon red and yellow eyes blind me.
Anger is looking at me with his glowing eyes.
I hate it.
It won't leave me alone.
Anger smells like rotten eggs and sour milk on my tea.
Anger shoots like lightning over the sea.
It scares me.
It's screeching, slowly louder and louder.
I run as fast as I can but it follows me.
He shrieks, 'You can't run away!'

Robbie Murray (9)
Appledore Primary School, Bideford

Anger

Anger moves as fast as a cheetah,
And sometimes crawls around like a house cat.
Anger starts off as small as a crumb,
And grows as big as a shark through the day.
His eyes are black and blue as if he has been punched.
Anger tastes like rotten eggs.
Anger smells so rotten like milk gone off!
Anger roars like a lion,
Anger's touch is a thump.
It frightens me!

Billie Knowles (9)
Appledore Primary School, Bideford

Footie Match

F ootball crazy, football fun
O ff he goes as he gets a red card
O ff he goes and on comes Rooney
T rips up and gets a penalty
B ad tackles is my game
A rranging teams as they run
L osing matches I can't do
L iking football is all I can do.

Jake Dascombe (9)
Bickleigh-On-Exe Primary School, Tiverton

Two Times Tables

Two tigers tearing teacloths.
Four fish fighting.
Six serpents saying silly words.
Eight elephants eating eels.
Ten turtles telling tales.

Connie Yeoman (10)
Bickleigh-On-Exe Primary School, Tiverton

Cat

Dog tormentor
Rat racer
Mouse slayer
Bird killer
Rain hater
Tree climber
Wool player
String lover
Sleep crazer
Food fazer
Excellent cuddler
Brilliant snuggler
House roamer
Puppy framer
Kitten maker.

Kimberley Meech (10)
Bickleigh-On-Exe Primary School, Tiverton

Summer

In the summer
Sun comes out
There's hotness in
The air
Everyone goes
Out to play
In the fresh air.
On holiday
You hear
Late at night
The nightclub.

Kathryn Letheren (9)
Bickleigh-On-Exe Primary School, Tiverton

Who Is It?

Shoe nicker
Cat chasing monster
Puppy giver
Tail hitter
Grass eater
Mad licker
Great smeller
Paw-print maker
Nose nuzzler
High jumper
Loud barker
Scratch marker.
Dog.

Sarah Weber (10)
Bickleigh-On-Exe Primary School, Tiverton

Horse

H ay eater
O ver high bucker
R ocket racer
S harp seer
E normous fusser.

Luke Chanin (10)
Bickleigh-On-Exe Primary School, Tiverton

Bat

B lind as a bat
A crobatic as a cat
T errifying as a rat.

Ben Colston (9)
Bickleigh-On-Exe Primary School, Tiverton

Winter

Brown leaves covered in snow.
Oh how the wind does blow.
North, east, south and west
Oh how winter's my very best.

In winter all around
Snow is falling on the ground.
The snow is melting
Spring is showing
For now I have got to go.

Tanith Gould (9)
Bickleigh-On-Exe Primary School, Tiverton

Axes

Man musher,
Bone crusher,
Shield smasher,
Blood spiller,
Everything killer,
Face slasher,
Human murderer,
Head slicer,
Chest chopper . . .
What a whopper!

Alex Parslow (10)
Bickleigh-On-Exe Primary School, Tiverton

Football

Football is so cool.
Tackles, penalties and goals
Lots of playground fun.

James Collard (10)
Bickleigh-On-Exe Primary School, Tiverton

Winter

W ind is now blowing
 I cy footprints on the ground
N ew Year coming
T rees are now bare
E veryone's busy
R eindeers at work.

Alexandra Dudley (9)
Bickleigh-On-Exe Primary School, Tiverton

Winter

Snowflakes falling
Winds are blowing
Robins flying
Skies are dim
Fires burning
Presents under the tree
For me
That's the frosty winter.

Charlotte Alsopp (9)
Bickleigh-On-Exe Primary School, Tiverton

Axe

Man crusher
Shield smasher
Blood spiller
Tree crasher
School masher
Chest chopper
Chicken basher
Head sucker.

Andrew Bennett (10)
Bickleigh-On-Exe Primary School, Tiverton

A Dog

Cat chasers.
Rabbit racers.
Tail waggers.
Claw daggers.
Lawn clippers.
Jaw nippers.
Fast lickers.
Hole diggers.
Good runners.
Cat stunners.
Footprint makers.
Bone takers.

Lorna Callahan (10)
Bickleigh-On-Exe Primary School, Tiverton

Rule Breaker

Rule breaking,
Trouble faking,
Wimp hating,
Bully baiting,
Window smashing,
Car crashing,
Rule breaker.

Robbie Williams (10)
Bickleigh-On-Exe Primary School, Tiverton

Dragon

D eadly daggers
R avenously rampaging
A irborne acrobatics
G reen, glaring, glowing eyes
O ver valleys and villages
N ight hunting.

Adam Farr (11)
Bickleigh-On-Exe Primary School, Tiverton

Peacock

P eacock
E yes
A s
C oloured as the rainbow
O range, red, pink and blue
C ooling down in the rain
K aleidoscope walking.

Lauren Wiggins (10)
Bickleigh-On-Exe Primary School, Tiverton

Kitty

Dog teaser
Miaow maker
Mouse chaser
Tree climber
Milk lapper
Speedy bolter
Night creeper
Heavy sleeper.

Peter Wright (10)
Bickleigh-On-Exe Primary School, Tiverton

Clovers

Down by the river
Is a field,
A blanket of
Dark lush clover,
Crammed with green
Four-leaved stems,
Well named lucky
Meadow.

Kyrin Wiggins (10)
Bickleigh-On-Exe Primary School, Tiverton

Horse Show

H orses are fun
O ver the jumps they go
R ound the gymkhana poles
S ome people falling off
E arly in the morning preparing for the show.

S hows are fantastic
H orses look smart
O ver jumps and around the field
W inning cups and rosettes.

Chantelle Reid (10)
Bickleigh-On-Exe Primary School, Tiverton

A Horse

Carrot eater,
Silent sleeper,
Wind racer,
Stable pacer,
Ditch jumper,
Ground thumper,
Foal producer,
Sore loser.

Cathryn Buechel (10)
Bickleigh-On-Exe Primary School, Tiverton

Shark

S cary shark.
H orrible maneater.
A blood sensor
R azor-sharp ripping teeth.
K iller!

Rhys Faram (10)
Bickleigh-On-Exe Primary School, Tiverton

The Girl Who Hated Clocks

There was a young girl from Hong Kong.
Who hated the clock's little gong.
For she said it was bad, and the cuckoo was mad,
So why don't all clocks go wrong?

Emma Hird (10)
Bickleigh-On-Exe Primary School, Tiverton

Rhyme Haiku

A cat had a mat
Sat on the mat to wait for
A great fat slow rat.

Tom Huxtable (10)
Bickleigh-On-Exe Primary School, Tiverton

Football Haiku

It is the cup match
Sing the National Anthem
Two teams play to win.

Eddie Knowles (10)
Bickleigh-On-Exe Primary School, Tiverton

Harvest Prayer

A ll children have rights.
L et us express our opinions.
L isten to what we have to say.

C hildren are just as important as adults.
H elp us with our problems.
I f we are disabled, either in body or mind, don't treat us
L ike we're different.
D o not leave us.
R ights are rules.
E very child needs freedom.
N othing is as important as us, and our families.

H enry, Yair, Yoko, Mohammed,
    every one of us shall have a name and land to call our own
A lert us when something happens.
V alues of children are all around love.
E very child in every country should have rights.

R ights are for everyone.
I n times of war, shelter us and protect us from all harm.
G ive us food and clean water.
H eal us when we get wounds.
T reat us when we are ill.
S o stop it Sudan!

John Leaver (9)
Bishops Tawton CP School, Barnstaple

Today I Feel . . .

Pleased as a little girl playing
Fit as a cheetah running through the trees
Keen as I am about art at school
Hot as the lovely sun
Bold as James Bond on a mission
Bouncy as a pink bouncy ball
Keen as a cat purring
High as a giraffe eating leaves
Bright as a sunflower shiny and yellow
Light as a feather that's really colourful
Fresh as a freshly baked bit of bread
Sharp as a white shark's tooth
Warm as a desert
I'm so happy - I'm just lost for words!

Emily Brice (8)
Bradley Rowe Middle School, Exeter

Today I Feel . . .

Pleased as a puppy with a bone in his mouth
Fit as an arm wrestler
Keen as a fish swimming in the sea
Hot as a burning desert
Bold as a brave girl
Bouncy as a pogo stick
Keen as a cat purring for some milk
High as a tall mountain
Bright as a star sparkling in the sky
Light as a white feather
Fresh as brown baked bread
Sharp as a pointy knife
Warm as a radiator on number five
I'm so happy - I'm just lost for words!

Lauren Jenkins (8)
Bradley Rowe Middle School, Exeter

Today I Feel . . .

Pleased as a tiger called Tigger.
Fit as a hard-working grass cutter.
Keen as an agent girl.
Hot as someone in Australia.
Bold as a big, big elephant.
Bouncy as a hopping pogo stick.
Keen as a cat purring.
High as a beautiful blue sky.
Bright as a delightful little girl.
Light as a song projector.
Fresh as a clean bottle of water.
Sharp as a thorn bush.
Warm as a warm bed.
I'm so happy - I'm just lost for words!

Samantha Burnham (8)
Bradley Rowe Middle School, Exeter

Today I Feel . . .

Pleased as a girl playing football.
Fit as an arm wrestler.
Keen as a fish swimming in the tank.
Hot as a hot dog in a barbeque.
Bold as a scary lion.
Bouncy as a bouncy castle.
Keen as a Prime Minister.
High as a mountain really high.
Bright as a sun in the sky.
Light as a bag of cotton wool.
Fresh as an air-freshener.
Sharp as a pointy knife.
Warm as a furry bear.
I'm so happy - I'm just lost for words!

Sinead Cummings (8)
Bradley Rowe Middle School, Exeter

Today I Feel . . .

Pleased as a little girl with a bag of candy
Fit as a cheetah running through the trees
Keen as a little boy just about to do football
Hot as a hot dog on the barbeque
Bold as James Bond
Bouncy as a big ball bouncing in the air
Keen as a girl going swimming
High as a tower in the sky
Bright as flowers in the ground
Light as a kitten in a basket
Fresh as a new apple
Sharp as a pin on the floor
Warm as a puppy on your lap
I'm so happy - I'm just lost for words!

Ellie-Mae Bamford (8)
Bradley Rowe Middle School, Exeter

Today I Feel . . .

Pleased as a king with a crown
Fit as a chicken with short legs
Keen as a dog running round in a field
Hot as a brown pancake
Bold as Bob the Builder
Bouncy as a bouncy ball
Keen as someone going to Alton Towers
High as a twinkling silver star
Bright as a bright, yellow spotlight
Light as a scrambled egg
Fresh as a grape just picked
Sharp as a mountain top
Warm as a furry blue coat
I'm so happy - I'm just lost for words!

Oliver Moore (8)
Bradley Rowe Middle School, Exeter

Today I Feel . . .

Pleased as a bunch of roses to smell
Fit as a strong man with muscles
Keen as a kitten with a toy
Hot as a boiled egg
Bold as a lion
Bouncy as Bob the Builder
Keen as a dog with a bone
High as a castle
Bright as a sun in the sky
Light as a fish in the sea
Fresh as a just picked apple
Sharp as a shark's tooth
Warm as a sausage roll
I'm so happy - I'm just lost for words!

Danielle Framingham (8)
Bradley Rowe Middle School, Exeter

Today I Feel . . .

Pleased as a boy playing football.
Fit as a leopard running.
Keen as a pig rolling in mud.
Hot as someone eating a pasty.
Bold as a bear fighting.
Bouncy as someone jumping on a bouncy castle.
Keen as me laughing.
High as a tall castle.
Bright as a shiny padlock.
Light as a goldfish swimming.
Fresh as a chicken laying an egg.
Sharp as a shark's fin.
Warm as someone in bed with a blanket.
I'm so happy - I'm just lost for words!

Ryan Challice (8)
Bradley Rowe Middle School, Exeter

Today I Feel . . .

Pleased as a boy playing football.
Fit as a cheetah running.
Keen as a climber climbing a thousand feet high.
Hot as a desert.
Bold as a bulldog.
Bouncy as a ball bouncing on the grass.
Keen as a snake hissing.
High as ten thousand four-hundred and twenty-one feet in the sky.
Bright as a butterfly in the sky.
Light as a shining sun.
Fresh as an apple just picked.
Sharp as a fishing knife.
Warm as a quilt on my bed.
I'm so happy - I'm just lost for words!

Joshua Jones (8)
Bradley Rowe Middle School, Exeter

Today I Feel . . .

Pleased as a clown
Fit as a cheetah in the forest
Keen as a football player scoring a goal
Hot as a pyre burning
Bold as The Rock wrestling
Bouncy as a grasshopper
Keen as a mountain climber
High as a skyscraper
Bright as a pot of treasure
Light as a pile of feathers
Fresh as an apple
Sharp as a knife
Warm as a radiator
I'm so happy - I'm just lost for words!

Dan Gallagher (8)
Bradley Rowe Middle School, Exeter

Today I Feel . . .

Pleased as a boy running
Fit as a man sprinting
Keen as a dolphin to go swimming
Hot as the sun
Bold as Bob the Builder
Bouncy as a bouncy ball
Keen as a footballer
High as a lot of clouds
Bright as a flower
Light as a feather
Fresh as a sausage roll
Sharp as dog's teeth
Warm as a sausage in a pan
I'm so happy - I'm just lost for words!

Tommy Morgan (8)
Bradley Rowe Middle School, Exeter

Today I Feel . . .

Pleased as a boy playing football
Fit as a lion eating chicken
Keen as a boy watching TV
Hot as a desert full of kangaroos
Bold as James Bond
Bouncy as a bouncy castle
Keen as piranha eating fingers
High as a giraffe chewing leaves
Bright as a shining sun
Light as a colourful moon
Fresh as an apple growing on a tree
Sharp as a butcher's knife
Warm as a fleecy blanket
I'm so happy - I'm just lost for words!

Keiran Brown (8)
Bradley Rowe Middle School, Exeter

Today I Feel . . .

Pleased as a monkey swinging in the trees
Fit as a lion running in the grass
Keen as a fish swimming in the sea
Hot as the sun in the sky
Bold as Bob the Builder working
Bouncy as a ball bouncing high in the air
Keen as a crocodile catching fish
High as a skyscraper in the sky
Bright as a flower in the garden on a bush
Light as a feather floating in the air
Fresh as a cup of water from a spring
Sharp as a pin in a sewing box
Warm as a radiator turned up high
I'm so happy - I'm just lost for words!

Shannon Hutchings (8)
Bradley Rowe Middle School, Exeter

Today I Feel . . .

Pleased as a monkey swinging in trees
Fit as a lion running in the jungle
Keen as a fish swimming in the sea
Hot as the sun shining
Bold as James Bond
Bouncy as a kangaroo in the wild
Keen as a rich king eating grapes
High as a hot air balloon
Bright as a blue car
Light as a kitten playing with a ball of string
Fresh as a banana on a tree
Sharp as a shark's tooth
Warm as a fresh laid egg
I'm so happy - I'm just lost for words!

John Lindsay (9)
Bradley Rowe Middle School, Exeter

Today I Feel . . .

Pleased as a bunny with some lettuce
Fit as a marathon runner carrying 200kg
Keen as a dog wanting a bone
Hot as a freshly cooked potato
Bold as James Bond
Bouncy as a rabbit in a field
Keen as a bear eating honey
High as a giraffe's tall neck
Bright as a sun in the sky
Light as a feather
Fresh as a freshly picked banana
Sharp as a knife
Warm as a freshly laid egg
I'm so happy - I'm just lost for words!

Jodie Vinicombe (8)
Bradley Rowe Middle School, Exeter

Today I Feel . . .

Pleased as a fuzzy bee.
Fit as a big giant.
Keen as a princess.
Hot as a hot oven.
Bold as a silly dad.
Bouncy as a swishy bouncy ball.
Keen as a prince.
High as a really big fluffy tree.
Bright as a shooting star.
Light as a green leaf.
Fresh as a loaf of bread in a shop.
Sharp as a shark in the salty sea.
Warm as a thick jumper.
I'm so happy - I'm just lost for words!

Charlotte Selley (8)
Bradley Rowe Middle School, Exeter

Today I Feel . . .

Pleased as dolphins
Fit as a running cheetah
Keen as a cat
Hot as a volcano
Bold as a big giant
Bouncy as a kangaroo
Keen as a dog
High as the sky
Bright as a light
Light as a feather
Fresh as a day
Sharp as a pin
Warm as a hot dog
I'm so happy - I'm just lost for words!

Adam Reed (8)
Bradley Rowe Middle School, Exeter

Today I Feel . . .

Pleased as a sinking feather
Fit as a speeding footballer
Keen as a goldfish swimming in his tank
Hot as a shooting star
Bold as a sun getting down
Bouncy as a trampoline
Keen as a bird building a nest
High as a long giraffe
Bright as a shining sun
Light as a sparkling star
Fresh as a bottle of milk
Sharp as a diamond in the sky
Warm as a hot bath
I'm so happy - I'm just lost for words!

Shannon Cole (8)
Bradley Rowe Middle School, Exeter

Today I Feel . . .

Pleased as a birthday cake.
Fit as a zooming cheetah.
Keen as a snowing hill.
Hot as chocolate melting in your mouth.
Bold as a giant killer whale.
Bouncy as a brown hopping kangaroo.
Keen as monkeys in their cage.
High as a giant building.
Bright as a bolting light.
Light as a boiling sun.
Fresh as a white egg.
Sharp as a sharp knife.
Warm as a warm shower.
I'm so happy - I'm just lost for words!

Lauren Woodcock (8)
Bradley Rowe Middle School, Exeter

Today I Feel . . .

Pleased as a shooting rocket
Fit as a leaping frog
Keen as a shooting star
Hot as a sun shining on my back
Bold as sun setting down
Bouncy as a jumping kangaroo
Keen as smiling fish
High as a fat giant
Bright as a glimmering shining star
Light as a silver moon
Fresh as the cool air
Sharp as a point pointing up
Warm as a sun shining hot
I'm so happy - I'm just lost for words!

Emily Cleave (8)
Bradley Rowe Middle School, Exeter

Today I Feel . . .

Pleased as Winnie the Pooh with honey
Fit as a cheetah
Keen as a bird building its nest
Hot as a shooting star
Bold as a painted up clown
Bouncy as a trampoline
Keen as fish in the sea
High as an aeroplane
Bright as a volcano
Light as a sparkling snow
Fresh as a new twisting slide
Sharp as a sparkling star
Warm as a twisting star
I'm so happy - I'm just lost for words!

Paula Hill (8)
Bradley Rowe Middle School, Exeter

Today I Feel . . .

Pleased as a cold snowball
Fit as a zooming monster
Keen as a spotty, frozen ice man
Hot as a big cooker
Bold as an old man with no hair
Bouncy as a kangaroo bouncing in the air
Keen as a man with big large hood
High as a big brown large tree in the air
Bright as a zooming star
Light as a candle on a table sparkling
Fresh as a fresh hot dog
Sharp as a shark's teeth swimming in the sea
Warm as a hot, boiling candle
I'm so happy - I'm just lost for words!

Sophie Ball (8)
Bradley Rowe Middle School, Exeter

Today I Feel . . .

Pleased as a booming cheetah
Fit as a boxing man
Keen as a chocolate melting in my mouth
Hot as spicy bacon
Bold as the deep blue sea
Bouncy as a zoomy footballer
Keen as a frozen monkey
High as Alton Towers' Oblivion
Bright as a shooting star
Light as a fiddly feather
Fresh as a juicy apple
Sharp as a shiny diamond
Warm as a comfy bed
I'm so happy - I'm just lost for words!

Ryan Harding (8)
Bradley Rowe Middle School, Exeter

Today I Feel . . .

Pleased as a shooting star up in the blue sky
Fit as a monkey in a tree that goes zooming
Keen as a goldfish big and dim floating in its bowl
Hot as a sausage sizzling in a pan
Bold as an elephant with a long trunk
Bouncy as a trampoline
Keen as a bird building its nest
High as a skyscraper so high in the blue sky
Bright as a sun so red
Light as a shining star
Fresh as a white egg
Sharp as a bit of glass
Warm as a fire in the house
I'm so happy - I'm just lost for words!

Chloe Reed (8)
Bradley Rowe Middle School, Exeter

Today I Feel . . .

Pleased as a speedy cheater
Fit as a fuzzy dog
Keen as a pretty girl
Hot as a steaming engine
Bold as a giant killer whale
Bouncy as a bouncy Tigger
Keen as a man with a big hood
High as a big bike
Bright as a blond kitten
Light as a light bulb
Fresh as a bottle of milk
Sharp as a big needle
Warm as a tumble drier working all day
I'm so happy - I'm just lost for words!

Jaid Spinks (8)
Bradley Rowe Middle School, Exeter

Today I Feel . . .

Pleased as a party popper
Fit as a football player
Keen as a new friend coming into school
Hot as a big brown cake
Bold as the deep blue sea
Bouncy as a football
Keen as a cousin coming into school
High as a skyscraper
Bright as a twinkling star in the sky
Light as a big light bulb
Fresh as a juicy orange
Sharp as a thick pin
Warm as a big fire
I'm so happy - I'm just lost for words!

Laura Rogers (8)
Bradley Rowe Middle School, Exeter

Today I Feel . . .

Pleased as a shooting rocket
Fit as a fast cheetah
Keen as a shooting star
Hot as sun shining on me
Bold as sun setting down
Bouncy as a bouncy kangaroo
Keen as a prince
High as a fat giant
Bright as a glimmering star
Light as a silver moon
Fresh as cold air
Sharp as a shooting diamond
Warm as a thick jumper
I'm so happy - I'm just lost for words!

Stephanie Lambshead (8)
Bradley Rowe Middle School, Exeter

Today I Feel . . .

Pleased as a juggling ball
Fit as a footballer
Keen as a dolphin
Hot as hot dog
Bold as elephant
Bouncy as a kangaroo
Keen as a dog
High as a skyscraper
Bright as a lamp
Light as a sky
Fresh as a chicken
Sharp as a piece of glass
Warm as a cat
I'm so happy - I'm just lost for words!

Aron Hutchings (8)
Bradley Rowe Middle School, Exeter

Today I Feel . . .

Pleased as a birthday cake
Fit as a monkey on an exercise machine
Keen as a starfish lying on a rock
Hot as a chick who is really mean
Bold as a blue whale
Bouncy as an orange basketball
Keen as a cat
High as a palace that is bigger than a church
Bright as a diamond in the sky
Light as a feather floating from the air
Fresh as a mouthwash that is in the bathroom
Sharp as a knife that is sparkling in the wash
Warm as a dove that is in his nest
I'm so happy - I'm just lost for words!

Lauren Evans (9)
Bradley Rowe Middle School, Exeter

Today I Feel . . .

Pleased as a monkey swinging
Fit as a climbing snake
Keen as a king counting his gold
Hot as the sun shining
Bold as a lion roaring
Bouncy as a bouncy ball
Keen as a crocodile catching fish
High as a skyscraper in the sky
Bright as a light bulb
Light as a feather
Fresh as a cup of water
Sharp as a pin in a sewing box
Warm as a radiator
I'm so happy - I'm just lost for words!

Katie Mundell (8)
Bradley Rowe Middle School, Exeter

Recipe For A Sphinx

Take a mane from a ferocious fierce lion
An udder from a mad and crazy cow,
And the flame and tail from a fire breathing dragon.

Add the growl from a dangerous tiger,
The legs from a cautious bull,
And the eyes from a slithery snake.

Decorate by putting blue food dye on tail,
Plait the ferocious fanning lion's mane,
And put donkey horseshoes on the bull's feet.
Put in a boiling hot cauldron and cook for five thousand years
(Stir five times a day)
And you will have made the Sphinx.

Mary Elsie Hawkins (10)
Bratton Fleming Primary School, Barnstaple

Recipe For A Chimera

Take the clawed paws of a frenzied wolf,
The black wings of a dark angel,
And the fur of a tortured tiger,
Add the mind of the devil himself,
Also the head of a disorientated Norn,
And the temper of a giant serpent,
Decorate with eyes of flame,
Diabolical claws of silver,
And the breath of a maddened dragon,
Stir in the tail of an unspeakable horror,
Put in a scorching oven,
And roast for eleven centuries,
And you have made a Chimera.

Silas Clay (9)
Bratton Fleming Primary School, Barnstaple

A Recipe For A Gorgon

Take a head from the ugliest troll on Earth,
A heart freshly removed from a bloodthirsty vampire
And thirteen venomous serpents for hair.

Add two, tiny, glaring scarlet eyes,
A body from a deadly devil
And a ghostly white flowing cape.

Decorate with a curvy chalk-white nose
A mouth as fiery as lava
And horribly crooked hands.

Stir in a pot of ice-cold dribble
And a spoon of rolling maggots
Bake for four thousand years
And you have made the Gorgon.
Beware!

Florence Cotten (10)
Bratton Fleming Primary School, Barnstaple

Recipe For A Minotaur

Take an angry bull's head,
A muscly caveman's body and scaly slimy snakeskin
Add a devil's scratching horns,
Horns like two sharp daggers
And a mane of bloodsucking worm.

Decorate with evil wild cats eyes and gigantic dribbling snakes mouth
Add decaying mummy's feet.
Stir in sick smelling dog's breath,
Put in a very hot oven and bake for a hundred years
And you have made the Minotaur.

Luke Thorne (9)
Bratton Fleming Primary School, Barnstaple

A Recipe For A Minotaur

Take a ram's haunting horns,
A red-hot buffalo's head,
And a killing breath of a deadly dinosaur.

Add my dad's dirty hairy legs,
A strong man's chest (or two!)
And cheesy feet that haven't been washed.

Decorate with bloodshot flammable eyes,
Teeth that scare the life out of you,
And skin as scaly as a crocodile.

Stir in blood red hair,
Place in an oven at gas mark 100
Cook for four hundred thousand years
And you have made a Minotaur.

Vashti Cotten (9)
Bratton Fleming Primary School, Barnstaple

Recipe For A Sphinx

Take a demon's head of flaming hot fire,
Eyes made of scarlet red marble,
And teeth made of ice-cold iron spears.

Add a rearing stubborn body,
With bones made of steel
And solid dagger-shaped hooves.

Decorate with a mane of stinging, violet flames
A mean devil's tail that shoots poisonous arrows,
And spit that carries deadly venom.

Stir in breath that could kill you at one hundred paces,
Put in the freezer, and freeze for a hundred years, no more, no less,
And you have made the Sphinx, so beware!

Sara Beth Ling (10)
Bratton Fleming Primary School, Barnstaple

Recipe For A Siren

Take three vicious heads,
A top of a pointy spear
And necks like tree trunks.

Add lots of spiky hairs,
Teeth as sharp as a knife
And a wobbly tail.

Decorate with long noses,
Eyes that sparkle in the sun
And claws that could rip the world apart.

Stir until there is a terrible smell,
Put in a huge dog's body.
Bake for millions of years
And then you have made a Siren.

Jack Mullen (9)
Bratton Fleming Primary School, Barnstaple

The Siren

Take a devil's bad-tempered cat body,
Three horrid dog heads and some very long necks
And a demon's ugly tail will do.
Add two, beastly bad blood eyes,
Ten dagger smelly toes and twenty rotten teeth,
And three, horrid sloppy ears.
Decorate with cows' blood and one hundred and twenty stinky hairs
And a horrid scale tail.
Stir in stink bombs and gas breath
With some of the horrible food in the world and lots of red.
Put it in a freezer for one hundred years,
Wake it up with a scream and you have made yourself a *Siren!*

Sophie Land (10)
Bratton Fleming Primary School, Barnstaple

Recipe For A Harpy

Take the enormous ears of an elf
And white hot hair from a witch's cauldron
And the sharpest needles from granny's sewing kit.

Add the decaying scaly wings of a vulture
And the flesh eating beak of a pelican
And spikes from a porcupine.

Decorate with dangerous blood-red feathers
And the mane from a gigantic lion
And the ice blue legs of a scary spider.

Stir in poisonous gas from deep within the ground
And tears as cold as ice
And salty sweat from a hanged man.
Bake in a stove for two hundred and eighty-four years on high
And you have made the Harpy.

Lydia Huxtable (9)
Bratton Fleming Primary School, Barnstaple

Recipe For A Sphinx

Take a fire-breathing head of a lion,
Skin as hot as chillies and an ice-cold body of a cow,
Legs of crunched up human arm bones
And a tail as sharp as a dagger going through your heart.
Add five spoonfuls of mayonnaise
And two spoonfuls of sugar to make it sparkle like lightning.
Decorate it with colouring for cakes
And make a mad face, not too mad.
Stir in strawberry yoghurt
And put on Gas Mark 10 for ninety-nine years
And you will have made a Sphinx.

Lily Northam (9)
Bratton Fleming Primary School, Barnstaple

Recipe For A Cyclops

Take a warty wrestler's wrist
And a clanky caveman's club.
After, fit in a thousand children's eyes,
Add some slushy sea-waved hair,
A groany moany voice
And bony blunt fungus feet.

Decorate with a shadow of a ghost,
A cloth of dangerous dust,
And bones made of stainless steel.
Stir at a hundred miles an hour
Then cautiously put in an oven
Which is boiling, burning hot
And bake for four thousand years, no longer, no less
And you have made an ancient Greek Cyclops.

Holly Ling (10)
Bratton Fleming Primary School, Barnstaple

Recipe For A Cyclops

Take an evil eye of a giant,
A caveman's club with a nail in it
And the muscles of a blood covered boxer.
Add a heart of an evil soldier,
Long gory intestines filled with blood
And veins of a hungry dog.

Decorate with an eyebrow made of rabbit hairs,
Fiery feet like frogs,
Toenails as big as windows.
Stir in snot from a crying baby,
A witch's nose.
Cook for one thousand years,
You have made the Cyclops.

Tim Huxtable (10)
Bratton Fleming Primary School, Barnstaple

Recipe For The Sphinx

Take a vicious male fire-breathing lion head
And a horse's body as strong as steel.
A malignant cow's udder and the devil's tail.
Add fire to the jaws of the lion's head,
Four legs from a swift spotted cheetah
And some sharp teeth of a leopard.

Decorate with red-hot lava eyes,
Have some anacondas for a mane
And a nose of a sly filthy fox.
Stir in hair from a woman's head,
Put in Ice Age conditions,
Leave for three million years
And you have made an ancient Greek monster
Called the Sphinx.

Matthew Essery (10)
Bratton Fleming Primary School, Barnstaple

Recipe For A Siren

Take three gruesome dog heads,
A scaly dragon tail with bright green speckles
Add some dog's breath,
Then add some vicious blue wolf veins,
Then add two fur necks and one lumpy neck.

Decorate it with black and brown fun,
Put on some skin as hot as chilli peppers
And some flesh on some of its teeth.
Stir in some ice-cold blood, a brain and two eyeballs.
Put it in a scorching hot oven and bake for two hundred years
And you have made the Siren so *beware!*

Natalie Clarke (9)
Bratton Fleming Primary School, Barnstaple

Recipe For A Cyclops

Take an ugly one-eyed sea monster's face,
A tub of slimy spaghetti
And muscles of a top class wrestler.
Add the blood of a python,
The heart of a dead man
And the thud of a mincing machine.

Decorate with slimy, greasy skin,
The colour of dark green
And the eyebrow of a dead sailor.
Stir in the breath of a demon
And place in a cauldron.
Bake for one hundred years
And you have made a Cyclops.

James Thomas (10)
Bratton Fleming Primary School, Barnstaple

A Recipe For A Siren

Take the three heads of a giant man-eating dog,
Razor-sharp fangs like bulls' horns
And jaws as strong as titanium steel.
Add super rough fur like jagged rocks,
A serpent's tail and red lava eyes.

Decorate with powerful supersonic ears,
A roar like an ancient horn
And a tongue that stings like a stinging nettle.
Place in the oven and cook for thirty thousand years,
Stir every twelve months
And you have made the ancient Greek Siren!

Charlie Rooke (10)
Bratton Fleming Primary School, Barnstaple

Recipe For A Minotaur

Take a flaming mad bull from a cramped cracked cage
And put its head on the world's strongest mad man.
Also take a pair of razor-sharp horns off an antelope,
Add a pair of great big sheep ears and a lion's mane
And some of the dreaded dragon's breath.

Decorate with ragged flowery shorts
And some roaring lion's teeth,
Also a tiger's voice.
Put in a freezing, frozen freezer
And freeze for four thousand and four years and twenty-eight days
You have made a Minotaur.

Johnathan Shapland (9)
Bratton Fleming Primary School, Barnstaple

Time To Get Up

Why must it be time to get up?
I'm tired, cold, bruised all over,
I can hardly walk.
I'm poor, poor, poor and only seven
I'd be better up in Heaven.
My life is a miserable horror,
It will soon be time for me to climb,
Time to go up the chimney once again.
Up the chimney I go,
I can hardly breathe and it's,
So dark, gloomy, sooty and so dusty I could suffocate up here.
It's like I'm in a house a small old house,
As cramped as a mouse.
The chimney's polluted with dust and my skin is like crust.
The chimney's as black as witch's hair,
Why can't adults go up instead?
It's just unfair.
Oh why, oh why, must it be time to get up?
All I wanted was to be loved.
Why, oh why must it be time to get up?

Reuben Greenidge (10)
Brayford CP School, Barnstaple

Misery In His Eyes

Misery in his eyes,
Anguish in his legs,
Dejection in his knees,
Depression in his belly,
Despair in his feet,
Distress in his lungs,
Gloom in his shoulder,
Grief in his calf,
Heartache in his chest,
Weary in his arm,
Sadness in his face,
Worn out in his wrist,
Suffering in his fingers,
Unhappiness in his body.

Helen Thomas (10)
Brayford CP School, Barnstaple

Anxious Little Boy

Sad, sad, sad little sweep
Anxious little boy
Deadly soot is in his throat
Poor, poor little boy.
Choking and coughing all day long
Scared and tired he is.
Climbing up the chimney
Fearlessly gripping the wall
Cutting his knee
Sad, horrible, cramped chimney
Gritty and murky it is.

Ben Thorne (9)
Brayford CP School, Barnstaple

My Life

I wake up
And my arms and legs are
Aching, I look around
It is dusty
I am really
Hungry.
I go to the house
And I start to climb up.
My feet are really stiff.
I climb and climb and climb
I slip and hurt myself.
I put salt on my
Knee, *ouch!*
I clean the chimney
And then go back
To a horrible home.

Pippa Byrne (9)
Brayford CP School, Barnstaple

Chimney Sweep

Tired and sleepy
Climbing like a monkey
Coughing and choking
Claustrophobic and cramped
Struggling and nearly falling
Dark as a bat
Horrible day
Sooty
Sad.

Sam Wildig (9)
Brayford CP School, Barnstaple

A Sad Life

A sad little boy
Climbing chimneys
Day in
Day out
Cramped in-between brick walls
Sooty mist flying about
Scared that he will fall
Deadly soot in his throat
Battered and bruised
A sad life it is.

Freddie Jones (9)
Brayford CP School, Barnstaple

Tired Little Boy

Sad, sad heartbroken boy
Anxious all the time
Tired
Exhausted
Ready to drop
Restricted like peas in a pod
In that gloomy and dark chimney
Such a tired little boy.

Chilli Small (8)
Brayford CP School, Barnstaple

Work, Work, Work, All Day Long

A tragic tiny boy
Hungry and tired.
Damp and miserable
Smelly and dirty
Wet and freezing.
Work, work, work all day long.

Willow Beauchamp (8)
Brayford CP School, Barnstaple

Tired Tear

Tired as a tear dropping down, down, down,
Anxious little boy in a chimney of soot,
Hurting your arms, knees and everywhere,
You're scared.
You want to go home to see your mother and father
But no, no, no.
The chimney is a sooty mist up through the house,
You climb to the top, you get out
But your parents
They're not there,
You want to be loved, loved, loved.

Terri-Anne Groves (9)
Brayford CP School, Barnstaple

In The Overcast Chimney

In the overcast chimney
Is a horrible place to be
Soot, soot, soot, soot sooty.
It makes your blood cold
It's as murky as mud
Chimney sweeps hate it
But they have to go up.

William Osborne (7)
Brayford CP School, Barnstaple

Poor Jack

Day begins for little poor boy Jack,
Off he goes with his sack.
Up the chimney he goes where it is dark and gloomy
It is scary and dark and cramped as a little mouse.
I don't get paid.

Gemma Heal (10)
Brayford CP School, Barnstaple

A Very Sad Life

Anxious little boy,
Murky as mud,
Deadly soot,
Sad and lonely,
Tired as can be,
Sooty mist,
Cramped in a small chimney,
Gritty and pity,
Horrible and dark,
Outrageously cold,
Creepy and crawlies,
Miserable and moody,
Colds and chokes,
A very sad life,
Bumps and bruises.

Bethany Pearson (9)
Brayford CP School, Barnstaple

Anxious Little Boy

Anxious little boy
Woke up feeling hungry
Got his dusty broom
Climbed the chimney
It was deadly
It was spooky
Murky as mud
Anxious little boy
Scared
Down the chimney
He wished he had his family.

Aaron Beauchamp (7)
Brayford CP School, Barnstaple

Sad Little Boy

Sad little boy,
Climbs the chimneys,
Sweeps the soot,
Cough, cough, cough.

Sad little boy,
Climbs down the
Chimney,
Cuts his knee,
Ouch, ouch, ouch.

Sad little boy,
Hungry and tired,
No more food,
Sob, sob, sob.

Sad little boy,
Wanted to be loved
I want parents,
To love, love, love.

Ben Jones (7)
Brayford CP School, Barnstaple

A Horrible Life

Anxious,
Cold-blooded child,
Friendless,
A cramped chimney.
Claustrophobic,
Murky as mud,
Deadly as soot,
A creepy chimney,
A horrible life.

Sarah Thomas (7)
Brayford CP School, Barnstaple

What A Miserable Life

Anxious little boy
Cold-blooded child
Climbs cramped chimney,
Claustrophobic,
Gloomy,
Dark as a night sky,
Deadly soot,
Murky as mud,
What a miserable life.

Connie Heal (7)
Brayford CP School, Barnstaple

Chimney Sweep

I woke up cold, tired and hungry
In my shadowy little room.
I walked down the stairs
Heading for my horrible day of gloom.
I climbed up the chimney into a black mass of soot.
I'm weary and tired. Where am I going to put my foot?
I go up, up, up. I can nearly see the lights. Oh I really don't
                                        like heights.
Why, oh why do I feel like I'm going to die?

Sean Dallyn (10)
Brayford CP School, Barnstaple

Poor Little Chimney

Gloomy, gloomy, gloomy up the tight chimney breasts,
I get paid nothing a day,
It's a terrible life being a chimney sweep.
My master is rich, but I sleep in a cellar.
It's tight and gloomy up the chimney,
Not much fun being a chimney sweep.
It's worse than the desert,
I think my master's horrible,
He sleeps in a massive room.

Oliver Maundrell (10)
Brayford CP School, Barnstaple

Chimney Sweep

Black pit
Scary work
Soot in my mouth
Cough, cough, cough
Lonely boy
Upset boy
Bruised boy
Hungry boy
Cold boy.

Jessica Furlong (7)
Brayford CP School, Barnstaple

In The Middle Of The Night

In the middle of the night
I look to see the bright moonlight
As I stroll through the trees
I start to feel a cold breeze.

Then suddenly the light glows
And the river beside me flows
Then suddenly the hot sun comes out
And I wonder through the trees about.

Then I make my way home
And then something rang, my phone
Only my mum
Saying to come home.

Natasha Murch (10)
Canada Hill CP School, Newton Abbot

Dead Of Night

The shimmering rays of the moonlight
Hit the rocky edge of the mossy cliff.
Standing on the wet grass
With a puddle of mud next to you,
Something scratching something
But what?
The bark peeling off the rustling trees
The full moon cutting through the trees like a silver blade
The sea smashing the battered rocks,
The wind whistling
Whilst the owl was gazing on
The erupting noise of thunder dominated the night.

Jacob Scotte-Hatherly (9)
Canada Hill CP School, Newton Abbot

The Cave

There up ahead a chink of light
The eerie sound of dripping from stalactite to stalagmite
The bats swooping and plummeting
The chink of light is growing closer . . .

Shadows swirling and dancing
Taking the form of whatever they feel like
Some shaped like beasts, some shaped like harmless creatures.
The chink of light is growing closer . . .

The strong smell of limestone wafting through the cave
The sound of footsteps sends a chill down my spine.
The chink of light is really close now . . .
And as I round the corner *argh!*

James Brookman (10)
Canada Hill CP School, Newton Abbot

In My Dream

One night I go out
I hear people shout and shout
As I go into the dark
I see people in the park
I see a house and I have a look
I hear squeaky floorboards as I walk in
Owls hooting in the icy cold night
Spooky ghost float around the room
Spiders crawling down the wall
Bats beginning to fall
I hear ghosts screaming
As I am dreaming.

Kamisha Adams (9)
Canada Hill CP School, Newton Abbot

The Bowerman's Nose

It was a perfect day for hunting
The tor was in good health
The hunter grabbed his deadly shotgun
Then headed away for south.

Up the tor he quietly climbed
His back carrying a sack
At the top of the tor he met some witches
The hunter was to go back.

He refused to go away
But then eventually did
He said he wouldn't go hunting tomorrow
But that was a very big fib.

Darkness was coming
The hunter raced home
Preparing for tomorrow
The witches would moan.

The witches cruel and tight plan
Was to turn the hunter to stone
If he returned the next day
They said in their croaky tone.

But then on the next day
The sun was beaming out a light
The hunter grabbed his shotgun
Unaware as ahead was a terrible fright.

The hunter clambered bravely up the steep and enormous hill
His hounds followed behind so fast
The witches waiting at the top
Ready for their cast.

The witches warned the hunter
What was coming very soon
An old trick they had planned so well
Under the glistening moon.

The scared hunter walked towards the granite
Nervously and slow
The cruel witches pointed their dark wands
The Bowerman's Nose is now a stone!

Jack Wotton (9)
Canada Hill CP School, Newton Abbot

Miles Of Darkness

Five miles down beneath the waves,
Where life has never seen the sun's rays.
Only the boldest,
Will reach the coldest.
The gloomy silence only broken by a flurry of fish,
A ghostly octopus seeks out his next dish.
There is never any light,
In this endless night.

Five miles up beneath the glistening moon,
Where I feel danger will loom.
The darkness of the wood comes ever nearer,
My thoughts become even more fearing.
I feel blind in the eerie dark,
And jump at a sudden bark.
The smell of damp leaves drifts to my nose,
As I walk through piles of leaves all in a row.

Five miles further in outer space,
Stars appear to have a race.
Different shapes, different sizes,
Some will fall, another rises.
Twinkling diamonds light the sky,
Glistening brightly up so high.
You are always there every night,
Burning strongly with all your might.

Daniel Henderson (9)
Canada Hill CP School, Newton Abbot

Alone In The Darkened Room

'Oh no,'
Here it goes again,
In the darkened room,
You'll never know,
What's going to happen?
A bomb might drop,
On my house,
I don't know?

But I know I'm safe,
Inside my room
Dark or no dark,
I'm safe,
Everyone has a,
Dim pitch-black
Behind my blackout,
Curtains until the war,
Ends.

Lois Gill (9)
Canada Hill CP School, Newton Abbot

The Creature's Cave

In the creature's cave I see
A frightening bat glaring down on me
Also in the cave I hear
Echoes where the waves are near.

In the creature's cave I feel
A sandy surface and rocky shells
Also in the cave I smell
Seaweed and something that I cannot tell.

In the creature's cave I see
The creature looking right at me
Also in the cave I see
Gushing waves pouring down on me.

Sophie Hyslop (10)
Canada Hill CP School, Newton Abbot

Fabulous Display

The huge tree scrunching and rustling in the dark,
Brightly coloured flames turning into sparks.

Under my boot it is wet and damp,
Owls hoot, as I get close to camp
I can see the bonfire sparks scattering
As the group of teenagers stand happily chattering.

Rainbows of colours flying up into the air
Making everyone stop and stare,
Loud noises like bombs going off
Leaving lots of smoke causing me to cough.

The huge tree scrunching and rustling in the dark
Brightly-coloured flames turning into sparks
Scarlet is a colour bright
Showing clearly in the night!

Jack Lewis (10)
Canada Hill CP School, Newton Abbot

Dad's Attic

I've gone to my dad's house today
And the only spare room is the attic
As I shiver
The damp musty walls close in on me
When I walk
The mysterious magical moonlight raised a path for me
While the floorboards snap at my feet.
It was then I peered through the window
And something took me by surprise
A flash and a bang and then, something dazzled my eyes,
The powerful but extraordinary colours
Start to fill me with fear
As I shut my eyes and ears
Suddenly it's all disappeared.

Megan Kingsley-Smith (11)
Canada Hill CP School, Newton Abbot

Starlight

In the dark night
With no lights burning bright.
The icy cold air gushing round
Dark looming trees standing ground.
Moonlight glaring down at you.
Leaves dancing with the wind,
And bouncing to and fro,
You can just see the flowers in a row swaying gently.
Then it starts, the rain again.
Coming pattering down in great lumps if you listen
Carefully you can hear their bumps
Shimmering stars up high come passing by.
The owls hooting on a branch
In the darkness of the night.

Fay Sawkins (9)
Canada Hill CP School, Newton Abbot

Walking In The Moonlight

As the stars sparkle in the sky
Me and my friend wonder why? Oh why?
All the glowworms are wriggling around
As we walk on the soft, soft ground.

The water in the sea is icy cold,
The colour of the sand is bright gold
The lighthouse beam is big and bright
As it searches through the night.

The full moon is shining bright,
As it guides people through the night.
Wind is blowing through our hair,
But neither of us has a care.

Luke Nicholls (10)
Canada Hill CP School, Newton Abbot

Leaping Shadow

Silence, cold and lonely streets
No lights just dark
No happiness in the atmosphere.

In my room tearful depressed
Angry, scared and frozen minds
Crying unable to run away.

Just sit . . . wait
Summer now - seems like winter
Gloomy in my room like no one.

Nothing to cheer me up
Waiting and praying for the all-safe sound
To be finally happy again until the shadow
Casts its spell on us again.

Rachael Guilfoyle (10)
Canada Hill CP School, Newton Abbot

Aircraft

Night-time comes, the sound of sirens start,
Aircraft fly around like a dragonfly that darts.
Spotlights flicker on like a show;
Planes zoom around through sunshine and snow.

The Home Guard gets out a great big gun,
After they shoot down a Heinkel, it's a job well done.
One Spitfire circles around being lazy
If he meets a Fôcke-Wulf, he'll be the one pushing up daisies.

VI bombs glide silently through the sky,
The blow up buildings after they fly
One by one aircraft drop;
Oh how I wish this war would stop.

James McGladdery (10)
Canada Hill CP School, Newton Abbot

Freaked Out In The Dark

I went to bed not a sound from my brother
Not my sister
Soon I fell into a good night's sleep
Then I started dreaming
More, then it got worse and worse
Then it was a nightmare
'No! No!' I said I said in my nightmare
Then suddenly *boom*
And I woke up
Then my head
It started to shake a bit
Then more and more
'No! No!' first a horrible nightmare
Now a splitting headache
But no it wasn't a splitting headache
It was worse, much worse
Then *squeak*, I stopped
Then again *squeak, squeak*
I thought about it
What could it be?
Then I started to cry very worriedly
Then was sick
Now I was really freaked out
So I cuddled up to my pillow
Until I found out it was gone!
Then *bang*
My door fell down.

Shannon Pitts (9)
Canada Hill CP School, Newton Abbot

Night Light

The swishing trees that rustle in the breeze
I feel the drizzle and hear the waterfall
The stars make the salt crystals flicker.

The night scented flowers that attract the exotic moths
That fly into me as I stand on the damp moss
The bats swoop round feasting themselves.

The glowing eyes that belong to the animal of the dark
Came at the same time as the footsteps
And firefly and glow worm display.

Then the dark held hints of light
As the dawn approached
The dawn was here and night was fading briskly.

I see the landscape that had surrounded me
During the long hours of darkness
I see the night animals returning home for the day.

I see the stalking cheetah
The maker of the footsteps and glowing eyes
Then the rush and then the kill.

Then I see the crystal clear waterfall
With it's narrow outlet flow
And salt crystals flicker in the rising sun.

The mossy ground with sand around
Is cool underfoot with the dew
The creeper swinging in the breeze swipes me gently.

The sunrise that sets the plains aglow
The rosy pink clouds lit by the sunrise
With not a single street light in sight.

Louise Hawkyard (10)
Canada Hill CP School, Newton Abbot

Followed In The Dark

The powerful rays of the moon
Beaming towards me,
Like a silver blade cutting
Through the trees.
Someone's near
Cliff top trees sway like skeletons
In the cold autumn wind.
A carpet of leaves crunching beneath me,
As I walk on towards the open space.
Someone's near.
Up in the black,
Shimmering stars dance.
Out in the blue,
I see the sea glistening.
Someone's near.
I stand on the brink of the cliff
And look down.
Too far to fall.
I look behind and all I see,
Is a long dark shadow,
That keeps following me.

Ryan Rogers (9)
Canada Hill CP School, Newton Abbot

Aeroplanes

Amazing aeroplanes flying through the sky
Like a really small prop plane floating through space
The rattle of engines and the lovely smell of the air
The beautiful look of the plane travelling through the clouds at speed.

The roaring of the plane taking off
The amazing views of the plane flying
The lovely noise of the plane's engines
The crackle of the brakes when the plane lands.

Matthew Fox (10)
Canada Hill CP School, Newton Abbot

A Dragonfly

A dragonfly, a dragonfly; following the river's edge,
Trying to break past the killer's ledge;
Struggling to get through the amazing fire,
A dragonfly a big fast flyer;

A dragonfly, a dragonfly; making the longest sigh;
Trying to beat the nightless sky,
Splashing past the windless air,
Into the nicest care;

A dragonfly, a dragonfly; staking out a German glider,
Whilst eating the tiniest spider;
Whipping past a cloudless sky, being a little shy.
After being a little sly;

Among the darts,
A dragonfly.

Thomas Sellick (10)
Canada Hill CP School, Newton Abbot

Inside Action

Massive machines making noises as they leave the ground;
People wondering what is going on back down on the
colossal ground
Hoping that when they land, there will be the
solid ground to step on once again.
People hoping the heavy trolley will come past, so they can eat
some special food.
They won't be starving because of the good solid food,
Thinking about the lovely food
Just anything, even some grain.

Now they are landing,
Suddenly, they hit the ground
And they're relieved to be safe on solid ground.

Glenn Stephens (11)
Canada Hill CP School, Newton Abbot

The Darkness

The loud hooting of the owls
The powerful wolf just howls and howls
The choppy breeze against my face
Me and my friends looking up at space.

The shadow birds dancing in the sky
What a sight, my oh my
The brightness of the window so far away
Lots of children have come to play.

The big dark trees just sway and sway
My best friend is here to stay
I can hear lots of echoes
Bouncing off the deep cold snow.

There are lots of cats with their green eyes
Looking up at me like I'm a piece of ice
Lots of stars in the sky
It's so beautiful, my oh my.

The loud hooting of the owls
The powerful wolf just howls and howls
The choppy breeze against my face
Me and my friends looking up at space.

Sam Kelly (10)
Canada Hill CP School, Newton Abbot

Flying High

I wake up in the morning and hear a buzzing noise
It's circling around the sky,
It's like a little creature,
But it's more like a small fly.

It's buzzing around all day and night,
A small slow plane attempts the sky,
And sparkles in the sunlight.

Laura Nott (10)
Canada Hill CP School, Newton Abbot

In The Cellar

The damp and dirty floorboards creaking
Rats and mice scuttering and squeaking
Cold wind wafting through an open vent
The moist and sticky cellar scent.

Wine and beer bottles standing tall
Cement crumbling out of the cellar wall
Mysterious footsteps from upstairs
Spooky webs floating like hairs.

The scary cellar door is creaking
As if the creepy thing is speaking
The spiders in their cobweb homes
Sitting on their home-made thrones.

Rusty, muddy gardening tools
Hanging from nails drilled in walls
Crates stacked up against the wall
Looking like they're going to fall.

The damp and dirty floorboards creaking
Rats and mice scuttering and squeaking
Cold wind wafting through an open vent
The moist and sticky cellar scent.

Ryan Partridge (10)
Canada Hill CP School, Newton Abbot

The Gloomy Street

Lonely I sat in a blacked out room.
In a house that was full of blacked out gloom.

I have not been able to go outside
I have to stay in so I can hide.

I want to go out so I can play
But mum said, 'It's not safe today.'

The aeroplanes may fly right by.
But they won't see me from the sky.

Hayley Gilbert (10)
Canada Hill CP School, Newton Abbot

I Stand Alone

I feel lost,
I'm full of grief,
I'm lost, alone.

In the dark all I see,
Are stars twinkling in the sky,
The shadow of a gigantic tree,
Glares down at me.

I feel lost,
I'm full of grief,
I'm lost, alone.

In the dark all I hear,
The crispy golden leaves rustling, rustling away.
The lark squawking, so deafening everyone can hear it,
To discover its beautiful sounds.

I feel lost
I'm full of grief,
I'm lost alone.

In the dark all I smell,
Is the musty stench of ancient whisky,
The fragrance of fresh red roses,
The whiff of an eerie bush.

I feel lost,
I'm full of grief,
I'm lost, alone.

Ben Fawcett (10)
Canada Hill CP School, Newton Abbot

Hitler Vs Churchill

In the moonlight glow
Hitler will try and blow
Up the United States
So off we go.

Churchill will be leading us
Through the stormy winds in England
With hardly any light
So fly away we shall.

We're approaching America
So stop them we shall
We're ready to shoot down the planes
But stop them we shall.

We're approaching Hitler's army
So shoot them we shall
We've got tanks, they've got planes
But will blow them all to Hell.

Churchill saw Hitler, so shoot him we shall
Germany turned back,
And friends we shall be
So back we go.

We've got fireworks
For the celebrations
Everyone's cheering
So back to England we will go.

Luke Keaveney (10)
Canada Hill CP School, Newton Abbot

The Door To The War

Bombs dropped like round fireworks,
Falling faster than raindrops
Black screens on the window
Tape on the doors with sacks,
No lights anywhere, everyone coming round saying
'Children, you leave tomorrow'
People crying, 'Fires, wires!
Nothing is working! Help?'
People scream!

Thomas Glover (9)
Canada Hill CP School, Newton Abbot

Fireworks

A big full moon in a dark black sky,
With little silver stars passing on by,
It wasn't cold on that night,
But what happened next was a real delight.
We sat at the table eating in the dark,
When suddenly there came a tiny spark,
And then it started a really amazing sight,
Fireworks booming in the night.

Imogen Uniacke (9)
Canada Hill CP School, Newton Abbot

The Storm

As the darkness came, it wrapped itself around the world.
Distant thunder, a storm is approaching.
As it arrived wind thrashed itself against the lonely windows.
The flashing lightning hit wailing trees
Clouds opened, rain thundered down on the creaking rooftops.
Far away an illuminated house glowed in the storm,
Welcoming anybody who sees it.

Edward Glanville (11)
Canada Hill CP School, Newton Abbot

The Evacuee

The city had been his home - forever!
Living in a slum.

Until one day without any warning
He got taken away.

He got taken to the countryside
A wide and open space

No shouting, no screaming, no bombing
Just a lonely, quiet, place.

Katie Mill-Gammin (9)
Canada Hill CP School, Newton Abbot

Little Frightly Manor

The haunted house is dark and scary
There's a monster inside who's very weary.

He's huge and fat,
And lives with rats
But what did he see? I wonder.

A little lad with dark plump skin
He's looking very very thin.

Kandi Noble (10)
Canada Hill CP School, Newton Abbot

The Frightened Boy

I am frightened
I have to sleep under my table
Every night
My next-door neighbours
Got hit by a bomb
Across the road was a bomb.

Katie Gale (9)
Canada Hill CP School, Newton Abbot

Aeroplane

A ladybird
Darting
Through the bright blue sky,
Spotty ladybird glistening in the sun
Its bright red wings shining in the sun.
Wondering what will come
Floating lonely in the sky
Like a dart doing what it likes as it heads for the bullseye.
Breaking through the air at top speed
Amongst the insects.

George Burton (9)
Canada Hill CP School, Newton Abbot

Aeroplanes

A butterfly darted very fast in the bright sky,
And whizzed past the other planes,
The colourful butterfly glistened in the sunlight,
And made a fantastic shadow.
Around its wings the dust was sprinkling with happiness
The flapping went really fast,
And gave the butterfly some fresh air!
Among them darted a butterfly.

Jordan Simpson (9)
Canada Hill CP School, Newton Abbot

My Blackout

Sun falls
All the rooms draped and curved with the thick black curtains
As I walk into walls as the dim light goes out.

Darkness now falls
I feel like I have been locked up in jail with nothing but *dark*
And not allowed out until the sun rises.

Lily Luscombe (10)
Canada Hill CP School, Newton Abbot

Spooky Dark

In the park it's very dark
Gigantic trees whistling in the wind, leaves swishing on the ground.

It must be bad to live in the dark in the park.

In the park it's very dark as the wind brushes the grass
After the leaves come first as they are the starter.

It must be bad to live in the dark in the park.

In the park it's very dark, foxes scrumming around,
Birds fluttering, as sudden move fireworks sight.

It must be nice to live in the park in the dark
With the brightening light of fireworks.

Abigail Hewings (10)
Canada Hill CP School, Newton Abbot

Up, Up And Away!

I look up at the sky
And there's an aeroplane zooming by.
But because it's so far up
It looks like a tiny butterfly.

It's zooming around,
Through the clouds,
It's gone . . . now it's found its way back
Now it's going to land.

Chloe Brown (10)
Canada Hill CP School, Newton Abbot

Evacuee

He believed he was living in a world of darkness
Scared and uncertain of what would happen next
Thought he was going to be drowned
When someone ran him a bath.

Gabriel Bailey (9)
Canada Hill CP School, Newton Abbot

All Alone

All alone,
By myself,
No one in the rooms,
Nothing on the shelf.

I used to feel,
So very calm,
With the comfort of my parents,
I'd come to no harm.

But now I'm crying,
I don't know why,
I feel so lonely,
Why oh why?

Right now I'm homesick,
I miss them so,
I feel so ill,
My tears, they flow.

My mum, my dad,
They must be scared,
They could be gone,
They could be dead.

The bombs I imagine,
Are constantly falling,
'Oh Mum', 'Oh Dad',
I'm constantly calling.

Oh Adolf Hitler,
I hate you so,
I hope you're going,
Down below.

At least I'm safe,
With no bombs or sparks,
At least I'm not hidden,
In the dark.

Aimee Myers (10)
Canada Hill CP School, Newton Abbot

In The Dark

It was a cold mysterious night
With all of the aeroplanes willing to fight.

All of the houses locked and shut
And all of the electricity has been cut.

Everybody was still and quiet
All of the aeroplanes were on a riot.

Once the aeroplanes have gone
All the bright lights were switched on.

Everybody went out of their houses
It was all silent just like a mouse.

People emerged from lots of places
There were quite a lot of happy faces.

Ben Ames (10)
Canada Hill CP School, Newton Abbot

The Spirits' Cave

In the musty cave I see,
A shivering bat glaring down at me,
His teeth are sharp I wouldn't go near.
He might react or fill me with fear.

I hear the noise of gushing water,
Plunging through a crack,
I wonder if the myth of legends,
Are true, if so, they're back.

Mysterious thoughts plunge into my mind.
The magical spirits are trying to hide,
I scream out loud, 'Just leave me alone.'
I wish, oh I wish I could just go home.

Emma Houdmont (11)
Canada Hill CP School, Newton Abbot

Night-Time Arrives

Night-time arrives,
The sound of Spitfires zooming into land,
Flashing lights, circling the sky
Gold and silver wings soaring through the mysterious cloudy night.
I hope this still goes on a brilliant flight!
I can smell smoke coming from the air above me,
I hope I don't crash into the deep blue sea.
There is a bomb nearby,
I hope I don't get hit and die.
I could hear crackling all around,
I hope I don't lose control and glide right into the ground
Quick I better get out my gun,
Then my work will nearly be done.

Joseph Richards (10)
Canada Hill CP School, Newton Abbot

The World Is Black

The world is black
As I lie in my cave of dark,
The world is blind,
As we live by dim candlelight.

The world is black.
As my light is swallowed by darkness
The world is blind.
As thoughts of war buzz round my head.

The world is black,
As I listen for the dreaded air raid siren
The world is blind,
Will the siren sound, will it, will it?

Beth Norrish (9)
Canada Hill CP School, Newton Abbot

In The Dark

It's 10.00 the sirens go off,
And mum comes in,
Turns off the light
Then shuts the door,
It's pitch-black,
I can hear the planes,
Overhead,
Dropping bombs,
On innocent people,
Some rushing to bomb shelters
Some rush to cellars,
Some stay,
Frozen with fear
They wait,
Then it's over,
Just like that,
Peace,
At last.

Heather Buttifant (9)
Canada Hill CP School, Newton Abbot

All Alone

All alone,
Nowhere near home,
I'm nearly there,
I forgot my teddy bear.

I'm in the countryside,
They've got a park and slide,
I'm all alone,
Nowhere near home.

All alone,
Nowhere near home,
I'm trying to be brave,
I feel like I'm living in a cave.

Josh Castree (10)
Canada Hill CP School, Newton Abbot

All Alone

I'm all alone in a house,
I do not even see a mouse.

I'm all alone, I'm nowhere,
In a stranger's home and lair.

I'm all alone on an old, old chair,
Without my mum and dad's care.

I'm all alone in the dark,
Hoping not to see a spark.

I'm all alone feeling sad,
Oh, I do know Hitler's bad.

I'm all alone living in Devon,
Who knows, my parents could be in Heaven.

I'm all alone lying in a sack,
Wandering if I'll ever get back.

Rachel Fogden (11)
Canada Hill CP School, Newton Abbot

In The Dark

It's dark, it's cold, the lights are out
All the aeroplanes are out and about.

The air is smoky, my lungs are filled
I know someone who was nearly killed.

Some houses were destroyed
People were very annoyed.

Children were crying
And people are dying.

I am in my room with my bear
And no one knew I was there.

Samuel Wakeham (11)
Canada Hill CP School, Newton Abbot

All Alone

I'm alone and scared
I've been torn from my family
I'm ever so scared for them
I want to go home
Me and my sister.

Me and my sister
She's so upset
We feel homesick
I'll never forget my mum and dad
Me and my sister.

I'll remember the warden coming for me
I had to run and get packed
I was so upset to leave
But I had to go
Me and my sister.

Lily Smith (10)
Canada Hill CP School, Newton Abbot

In The Dark!

It's dark and misty
I hear the buzzing sirens in my head
Waiting for the alarm waiting . . . waiting and waiting.
Alarm, alarm, the Germans are here
Turn the dim lights down.

I'm all alone in the dark,
I hear the bomber planes above me
Searching for me,
Waiting for me
Not knowing where I am
Is this my end?

Ashleigh Dummett (10)
Canada Hill CP School, Newton Abbot

Bombs And Terror

The darkness flies over the light
The darkness brings the German invaders at night,
To peace to horror, the sky turns grey.
Sirens go off, warning people to lie
Calm and draw their black curtains and turn every light off
Bombs hit houses setting them to burn,
Darkness makes people terrified.
Who is going to end this war?
Then the darkness creeps much further forward to us gazing
The fire engines put the sprinkling water
On the burning, blazing
The shooting bomb comes, we see their power
Houses bombed, the time has come.
Houses destroyed.

Rachel Craig
Canada Hill CP School, Newton Abbot

In The Darkness

In the dark all on my own with my family
I can hear the bombs going *boom* and people screaming, '*Help!*'

It's black, it's cold, and the air is dusty, aeroplanes flying overhead
The lights are out the air is musty
I can hear my friend, lying still cold.

Something has banged on the door
They are going to take me away, away, away.
I wonder oh why Hitler wants our life
Oh why? Oh why? Oh why?

Natasha Knott (9)
Canada Hill CP School, Newton Abbot

In The Dark

I'm in my house upstairs, alone
I can hear my wooden floorboards creaking,
Helicopters are above me,
I'm shocked,
Almost everything's fading
I'm hiding under my bunk bed.
Thinking of what to do,
It is cold, I am shivering,
I am frightened.
I'm here reading a scary book
Until I hear *bang!*
I thought it faded but no it hasn't
I'm really worried
I'm here upstairs alone.

Tarquin Warren (9)
Canada Hill CP School, Newton Abbot

In The Dark

It is dark, it is cold
And it is dirty.
It is windy it is noisy
And it is loud.
Like aeroplanes running
By and guns shouting
The lights are all out
The air is whispering and
Everything is getting blown up.
Everywhere I sleep,
There are flashlights from the distance
There are toys everywhere.

Oliver Hensberg (10)
Canada Hill CP School, Newton Abbot

In The Dark

Oh no! It's starting to rain
Oh help I hear a bomber plane
The noisy sirens are on
I hear the first dropping bomb.

The bomber plane is way up high
It's flying round in the sky
I'm being driven round the bend
Can this really be the end?

Jessica Powell (10)
Canada Hill CP School, Newton Abbot

The Way Of An English Fighter Plane

The aeroplane in the air almost fluttering by
Like a dragonfly, dropping a bomb on a tower,
Making trouble everywhere it goes,
Shooting by like a rocket,
High in the sky floating like a bird,
People like little dots on the ground,
All the lights off in the high street,
Aeroplanes all dropping bombs.

Matthew Frankpitt (9)
Canada Hill CP School, Newton Abbot

In The Dark!

Sirens I hear constantly,
Now the Germans show their bombing planes,
I see just black, just black I see,
I'm nervous and scared, what can I do?

My racing heart stops,
I take my final breath,
I wonder if this is the end?
Good-bye my fellow friend.

Josie Roberts (10)
Canada Hill CP School, Newton Abbot

In The Dark

I'm all alone in the dark
And my name is Mark.
My dad has gone to war
He has never left me before.

I hear a bang,
Where's my gang
I'm as scared as could be
Now it's just me.

My mum is called Josie
Her surname is Rosie
I hear a bomb
Now my dad has gone.

I start to cry
Because I think I'm going to die
I hear a plane
Now it starts to rain.

Kate Baverstock-White (10)
Canada Hill CP School, Newton Abbot

In The Dark

In the murky room pitch-black
Aeroplanes appear overhead
The lights are all out
There the musty air hovers about
I hear my fright battle the gusty cold
Everywhere aeroplanes bomb and destroy
Everyone silent
The air is dirty
I am hurt
The air raid is over
I'm lying in the dirt.

Stephen Powell (9)
Canada Hill CP School, Newton Abbot

The Poor Lonely Boy

The poor lonely boy
When World War came
The life of the slums,
Was torn apart into pieces
He got sent into the countryside to live
He tried to hide in the cattle farm
But he got caught
He was never the same again
His heart was torn apart into pieces.

Corin Yabsley (10)
Canada Hill CP School, Newton Abbot

In The Dark

It's black and cold and the dusty air floating around.
Aeroplanes flying over houses.
The lights are out.
The windows are blacked out.
Everyone is panicking
All I can hear is screaming inside of me
Then the siren went again.
They rushed to turn their lights off
They lay there silent - waiting.

Jade Steventon (9)
Canada Hill CP School, Newton Abbot

In The Dark

One night the German planes came
The sirens howl what a shame.
'Cover the windows, turn the light out,
Quick hide under the bed!' came a fierce shout.
I'm scared and cold, what a night
An enormous boom gives me a fright.

Connor Mantle (9)
Canada Hill CP School, Newton Abbot

Blackout

I've done my blackout
I feel like a shout,
I've worked all day,
And I really want to say
That I've finished my blackout.

I've done my blackout
Without a doubt,
There's a mess in every room,
I call it the house of doom,
But I've finished my blackout.

Guess what,
I've done my blackout,
Without a doubt
What shall I do?
Now that I've finished my blackout.

Brittany Caple (10)
Canada Hill CP School, Newton Abbot

In The Dark

I'm in my house it's calm and quiet
Waiting for the noisy sirens
Beep, beep, beep, beep
At that moment everyone's rushing
To turn off the lights quick, blackout, peace and quiet.
We're all huddled up together
Nothing in sight
Massive noises
Bang! very loud and I am scared
Bombs of Hitler
Made all this happen
Will we survive?
No one can forgive him
For I hope he goes below.

Bryony Larkin (9)
Canada Hill CP School, Newton Abbot

In The Dark

I'm in my house speaking to my mum
Suddenly the sirens went off
We hurry to blackout the windows
We light the smallest candle
We went into the shelter
My dad was in the war
We don't know if he's alive
Or dare I say it,
It was cold and dusty
My mum started to cough badly
It was pitch-black
Could not see anything
But the slightest light fading away
By the whistling of the wind
Coming through the thin wall
It's like I'm in a dream seeing things.
I'm seeing the German aeroplanes flying over us
Someone left their light on
The Germans are dropping their bombs on us.
Everyone listening, they wonder what's going on.
Bang!
Bang!
Houses were getting blown up, people screaming
Bodies everywhere
Phew it was only a dream
The aeroplane noises were gone
We went outside there was no damage at all
Everyone was safe and sound
Hooray
Hooray.

James Cluer (9)
Canada Hill CP School, Newton Abbot

Dark Shadow

In the cold, dark night,
Squelching beneath my feet,
Scared stiff, the smell of blood,
Never before.

In the cold, dark night,
The spooky noises,
Squeaks, whispers, croaking,
Never before.

In the cold, dark night,
Scuffling leaves underneath my shoes,
Cold, damp, wetting feel of the grass,
Never before.

In the cold, dark night,
A faint like ghost voice, goes straight past my ears,
An echo when I shout, but, in three different voices,
Never before.

In the cold, dark night,
Screeching of a big black bat,
A little eerie squeak of a mouse,
Never before.

In the cold, dark night,
A feel of a wet dog near my legs,
It was like I was in my own little box, I was trapped
Never before.

In the cold, dark night,
I could feel cold breath on my neck,
The shadow of a beast, the very dark shadow,
Never before,
For I, am never again.

Zoe Paddon (11)
Canada Hill CP School, Newton Abbot

Evacuated

The half wrecked home was his home for years.
Air sirens alerted for hundreds of children to be rushed off
In the countryside he could see cattle in herds of ten
And the sheep making queer noises thinking of lonely nights
And children in groups, so many sitting in a corner in the dark.

Seeing flames in the eyes of children, tears nearly
Bursting out like a hosepipe, with his suitcase
Swinging from side to side, he stumbles in the streets
Wondering if he will live the sound of bombs going off
And the screaming of the engines of planes in the sky.

Matthew Cole (10)
Canada Hill CP School, Newton Abbot

The Curse Of The Moon

Stars twinkling, fireworks crackling
With multicolours exploding in the air
The curse of the moon
Trees rustling, leaves crunching,
Golden leaves sparkling,
The curse of the moon
Ghostly sounds when in bed,
The chilly wind,
The mysterious owl tooting and hooting,
The curse of the moon.

Ben Roughley (10)
Canada Hill CP School, Newton Abbot

In The Dark

In the dark, alone, staying in my room
Waiting for the planes to go past, it is cold and dusty,
The blackout curtains make it dark so soon
The floor is hard and smells so musty.

When the sirens give their wail
Mum rushes in, I give my blanket a hug
I'm scared, I'm frightened, my face is pale
Mum picks me up and gives me a hug.

The planes have gone, peace at last
I crawl out from under my bed
We all rush out, the danger has past,
I see bodies on the floor lying dead.

Daniel Webber (9)
Canada Hill CP School, Newton Abbot

Disqualified

In the middle of the frosty day
I start to walk along the sandy bay,
I suddenly hear a crash of a noise
Of a crowd cheering, 'Come on boys.'

I walk to the front barrier,
Only to find the horse racers there,
I scream and shout
But it still does not count,
And my favourite man was disqualified.

Jennifer Robinson (10)
Canada Hill CP School, Newton Abbot

In The Dark

In the dark, people waiting,
For the bombs, hesitating.

Should they run should they hide?
Should they turn back on the lights?

It is pitch-black it's in the dark,
All the dogs forced not to bark.

The Nazis fly over, over the homes,
But the bombs have not yet been thrown.

The bombers are armed, the bombers are ready,
The bombs are perfect and the bombs are steady.

Still the blackout is over, the bombers fly past,
And that's another nasty Nazi attack.

George Morris (10)
Canada Hill CP School, Newton Abbot

The Blackout

Living with the blackout is not a pretty sight
It's black through the day, let alone through the night
There's things in my hair there's things everywhere,
That's living in the blackout!

Living in the blackout, hearing planes in the air!
It's hard to cope not seeing anywhere,
It feels like it's night all the time, it feels like you're stuck
In a clockwork rhyme, that's living in the blackout.

Liam Price (9)
Canada Hill CP School, Newton Abbot

Blackout

The name is Jack
The place is pitch-black
'It's going to be fine,' says Dad
But I have a feeling it's going to be bad
In this blackout it's very dark
There's not a sound in the park
After the blackout some of my friends are dead
Their bodies are covered in red.

Richard Maddison (10)
Canada Hill CP School, Newton Abbot

Best Friends

My friend is great,
She's such a good mate,
She always plays with me,
We always share our things,
And we like to sing,
My friend is great.

My friend is great,
She's such a good mate,
She always talks to me,
We always sit together
And we will forever and ever
My friend is great.

My friend is great,
She's such a good mate,
She likes to have fun,
We always scream and shout,
And laugh and run about,
My friend is great.

Abigail Maude (10)
Carclaze Junior School, St Austell

Fear

It is as black as the Devil's evil laugh
It is so loud it splits your head open and kills your spirit
It tastes as foul as reeking death.

So *evil* it smells of a rotting corpse that's one of its victims.
It looks like other devil's *evil eyes* and haunts you until you go insane

Feels like millions of spiders scattering over you,
                              biting and scratching,
It reminds me of something, I'm not sure of,
                    it is the very face of *evil, the Grim Reaper.*

Mark Delaney (10)
Crowan Primary School, Camborne

Tornado

I can destroy cities, eat rooftops,
And drink whole lakes,
Carry buses through their stops,
I can blow houses, hotels away,
And stay for the whole day,
Houses I can destroy,
When I'm mad I rant and rave
And never ever sleep through the day.

Christopher Vincent (10)
Crowan Primary School, Camborne

Happiness

Is like a glassy wave with a beautiful sunset on
The   horizon
It sounds like a blue bird tweeting
                              It tastes
Like a shiny watery water
                    Melon.

Jake Janes (10)
Crowan Primary School, Camborne

Dreams

A dream is multicoloured like a sparkling rainbow,
It sounds like birds in the breeze.
The taste is wonderful like blackberry and apple crumble
It's like a rose by your nose.
It looks like a peaceful garden,
Feels calm, calm as can be.
It reminds me of everything I said . . .

Oliver Hickey (10)
Crowan Primary School, Camborne

When I Am Grown Up

When I'm grown up I shall live off chocolate cake and sweets
And make my bedroom as messy as I could and never tidy it
I shall never come off the PlayStation
And I shall stay up all night watching TV
I shall spend lots of money on PlayStation games
And never eat fruit or vegetables again in my life
I shall never spend a day without playing rugby inside
And I shall own my own rugby pitch where my back garden would be.

Tom James (9)
Crowan Primary School, Camborne

Anger

Anger is as black as demons sucking your soul
It sounds like a banshee.
Tastes bitter like ash in your mouth
Smells like gas till it kills you.
Looks like Medusa till she gets you,
It feels like knives, stabbing your heart
Anger reminds me of fire burning me down till I'm calm.

Annabel Hawken (10)
Crowan Primary School, Camborne

The Stormy Sea

I can push their heads under the water so deep
Or I can sink a ship so they won't make a peep.

I can make a flood
Or I can splatter soggy mud.

I can dunk people under with just one wave
Or even push people down to a deep-sea cave.

I can be calm and quiet
Or I can make a huge riot.

Becki Kennelly (11)
Crowan Primary School, Camborne

Hate Is . . .

The colour of a litre of blood
It sounds like a lion roaring in a microphone
It tastes like your own sweat swimming in your mouth
It smells like a forest burning down.
It looks like me cut in half
It feels like your hand in a fire and kept there.
It reminds me of Hell, redder than ever.

Joshua Thomas (10)
Crowan Primary School, Camborne

Love

Love is *red* like a single rose,
It sounds like the kiss of happiness,
It tastes like spaghetti while you're sitting with the person you love,
It smells like romantic candles flickering in the moonlight,
It looks like your dreams but it's come true,
Tingling and happiness that's what it feels like,
It reminds you of the first day you found out you were in love.
That's love!

Lily Edwards (10)
Crowan Primary School, Camborne

Warning!

When I am grown up I shall play my music so loud
it will break the upstairs floor
When I am grown up I shall eat sweets for the rest of my life
I shall buy expensive football boots to impress my friends
And play football inside every room until I'm bored.
I shall play on my PS2 for weeks on end
And go out whenever I want
I shall invite all my friends over and have a giant sleepover
and have a big food fight.
I shall have a wrestling arena and play fight with my friends.
And I shall buy expensive beer
I shall wear tattered and battered old shoes
When I am grown up I shall not go to school
I shall be a giant and have everyone as my slave.
And I shall fight with my brother until he's on the floor
When I am grown up I shall be very unpleasant!
You won't want to be in my street!

Kieran Woolcock (10)
Crowan Primary School, Camborne

Happiness Is . . .

Happiness is pink as a rose in the garden
It sounds like snowbells on Christmas morn.

It tastes like the white chocolate melting in your mouth
It smells like the cooking of apple pie.

It looks like fairies dancing around you
It feels like you are lying on a Hawaiian Beach
With the palm trees blowing in the breeze.

It reminds me of my friends and family.

Shannen Barton (10)
Crowan Primary School, Camborne

The Giant Ant

Crashing through houses like Godzilla
Searching for food, crisps and junk food galore.
Feeling very sleepy, I lay on my neighbours' house!
Suddenly I awoke and yawned like one thousand ants.
Scared and lonely I crawl back to my house.

Oh, didn't I mention - I've been let loose in my mini model village.

Paul Fisher (10)
Crowan Primary School, Camborne

The Dragon

I can burn down cities
And cause such a stir
I can bully people
And singe animal's fur
I can eat mountains of food including spaghetti
When I'm in the mood I'm not so sweaty
So I am the dragon who breathes the fire.

Liana Goss (9)
Crowan Primary School, Camborne

Hurricane Ivan

I can pull out trees including their roots
Crush anything in my way with my humungous boots.

I don't want to harm anyone but I can give them a scare
I'm more frightening than any grizzly bear.

Then I die down my playtime's over,
Now I'm as scary as a four-leaf clover!

David Hilliard (10)
Crowan Primary School, Camborne

Penguin

Penguins like
Lovely snow
But when they walk
They're very slow.

But a few days later
It starts to ice
But they think
It's very nice.

They like to eat
Yummy yummy fish
They also like it on a dish.

Harry Edwards (8)
Crowan Primary School, Camborne

Meet The Devil . . .

I am the devil and extremely evil.
I will take over the world in a flash.
I live in Hell and it doesn't smell although it's all baked up.
I live and serve the Devil in a underground land.

Billy Reid (10)
Crowan Primary School, Camborne

Badger

Big badger
Crawling around in the dark
Crouching down
Going from his home forward and back.

No one knows
Searching for food
Sneaking in the gardens
With his wriggly toes.

William Henderson (8)
Crowan Primary School, Camborne

Flowers

I can give out a sweet scent
And have a stem straight or bent
I need watering or some rain
No others are the same.
I am pretty and I'm pink
When blue I help you think
I'm lavender and rose,
How many, no one knows
In gardens I am grown,
And I'm surely not alone,
There are tons and tons of me,
I am wild and I am free,
I am a flower.

Emma Winder (10)
Crowan Primary School, Camborne

The Baby

I can cry when I wish
For my favourite dish
My mum tells me off
When she's really cross
I can be good
When I really try hard
But I don't like the taste of *lard*
My horrible brother fed it to me
I ended up being sick just before tea
Can you guess what I am?
I'm as a quiet as a clam
I am the small cute baby!

Emily Masterton (10)
Crowan Primary School, Camborne

Cheetah

Cheetah speeds
Darting through the long thin grass
Then pouncing on its prey
As it wanders past.

Tails wave
In the air a lot
Like a cat with a toy
All covered in spots.

Rhys Fairlie (8)
Crowan Primary School, Camborne

The Wasp

I can make people die,
I can make men cry,
I can make an annoying noise
I have a killer voice.
I'm a big pest,
I don't ever rest,
I can go anywhere,
I do what I want,
I am a killer wasp.

Oliver McGeorge (9)
Crowan Primary School, Camborne

Anger

Anger tastes like a red-hot chilli sizzling in my mouth
It sounds like a base drum banging repeatedly in my head
Anger smells like smouldering ambers
It feels like volcanic rock
Anger can look red like blood
It reminds me of teachers when they shout.

Jennifer Booth (10)
Ellacombe CP School, Torquay

Darkness . . .

Darkness is bitter
Darkness is scary
Like the monster under your bed
Brown, black and hairy.

Darkness feels cold
Darkness is fearful
It reminds me of Hell
The Devil and evil.

Darkness is colourless
Not something to look through
Darkness is cold
Brown, black and blue.

If you are in darkness
Just use a light
And you will be okay
All through your nights.

Abigail Bratcher (10)
Ellacombe CP School, Torquay

Fun

Fun tastes like fizzy pop,
Fun smells like the summer air,
Fun sounds like laughter,
Fun feels like a soft teddy bear,
Fun looks like some balloons that you can pop,
Fun reminds you of snow falling.

Joanne Dudley (11)
Ellacombe CP School, Torquay

Fun

Fun tastes like something tickling you under your chin,
Fun sounds like people laughing every single minute of the day,
Fun smells like sweets and everything nice,
Fun feels like you have been given a talent from God,
Fun looks like some jelly that is stuck together and can never split up
Fun reminds me of all the things that I did when I was little.

Tennessee Mbbshir (10)
Ellacombe CP School, Torquay

Love!

Love is ruby red like a bubbling heart
It feels like confetti going down your back,
It tastes like blackberry pie
It looks like a love heart
It smells like rose,
It sounds like a humming bee,
It reminds me of my mum and dad getting married.

Ella Baillie (7)
Landscove CE Primary School, Newton Abbot

Anger

Anger is black like a vampire
It sounds like a gunshot
It feels like hot water
It tastes like wood
It looks like fire
It smells like junk
It reminds me of the dead.

Haze Curtis (7)
Landscove CE Primary School, Newton Abbot

Happiness

It looks like turquoise
Like green grass
It feels like floating silk in the sky
It tastes like a lollipop
It feels like running in the meadow
It looks like someone laughing in the sun
It smells like candyfloss
It sounds like playing children
It reminds me of the birds singing in the moonlight.

Rohanna Lang (8)
Landscove CE Primary School, Newton Abbot

Happiness

Happiness is a soft pink like the bright sunset
It feels like a golden feather drifting through the air.
It tastes like a delicious apple pie.
It looks like children playing in the sea.
It smells like sugary jammy donuts
It sounds like children playing in the swimming pool
It reminds me of snow falling on the ground.

Danielle Hayllor (7)
Landscove CE Primary School, Newton Abbot

Laughter

Laughter is pink like colourful stars
It feels like butterflies in your tummy.
It tastes like melted chocolate
It looks like people dancing in the night.
It smells like lollipops.

Daniella Gregory (7)
Landscove CE Primary School, Newton Abbot

Happiness

Happiness is like the sunset
It feels like a feather tickling on my face,
It tastes like a sugary dessert,
It looks like children playing at the seaside,
It smells like donuts with sugar on the top.
It sounds like children playing in the garden.
It reminds me of going to France each year.

Emma Holden (7)
Landscove CE Primary School, Newton Abbot

Laughter

Laughter is pink like candyfloss
It feels like floating in the air
It tastes like apple pie
It looks like laughter in the air
It smells like the hot sun
It sounds like girls giggling
It reminds me of my first day at school.

Abbie Irish (7)
Landscove CE Primary School, Newton Abbot

Laughter

Laughter is excitement like going to a mad disco
It feels like a dark exciting cinema
It tastes like pink and yellow sweeties
It looks like a dangerous game of football
It smells like gooey chocolate
It sounds like a flying V guitar
It reminds me of the Rolling Stones.

Rowan James (7)
Landscove CE Primary School, Newton Abbot

Laughter

Laughter is happy like bubbly candyfloss
It feels like you will never stop
It tastes like marshmallows
It looks like a sticky toffee apple
It smells like candyfloss
It sounds like popping popcorn
It reminds me of my mummy.

Georgia Leigh (7)
Landscove CE Primary School, Newton Abbot

Laughter

Laughter is blue like the sky
It feels like a warm day.
It tastes like bread and butter pudding
It looks like bubbles floating around
It smells like hot oozing soup
It sounds like music
It reminds me of my grandpa.

Angus Peachey (7)
Landscove CE Primary School, Newton Abbot

Anger

Anger is burning like flames inside my mouth
It sounds like burning bonfires
It feels like dead bodies underground
It tastes like flaming people
It looks like flames coming out of a bonfire
It smells like chocolate
It reminds me of monsters.

Matthew Samson (7)
Landscove CE Primary School, Newton Abbot

Love

I love the way the leaves fall down in the autumn.
It feels like newborn baby lambs being born
It tastes like a bunny eating a baby carrot
It looks like a wedding going on in a church
Its colour is baby-blue
It looks like confetti going on in a garden full of fireworks
It smells like lemon meringue cooking in the warm oven
It sounds like our family having a Christmas dinner
It reminds me of bubbling, popping and cracking fireworks.
It is a gift from God.

Hannah Carter (8)
Landscove CE Primary School, Newton Abbot

Anger

Anger is like a flaming fire
It sounds like a bullet being shot
It feels like being bitten by a wolf
It tastes like flames
It looks like a boiling bubbling spring bath
It smells like smoky gunpowder
It reminds me of big monsters.

Rosie Trott (8)
Landscove CE Primary School, Newton Abbot

Anger

It feels like red-hot burning coal in my tummy
It tastes like hot burning toast
It looks like an orangey red fire
It smells like car fumes in the air
It reminds me of my dad when he is late for work.

Jack Watson (9)
Landscove CE Primary School, Newton Abbot

Silence

Silence is black like a wasp constantly stinging you
It feels like a bee buzzing in your ear as if it desperately
                                        wants to get out,
It tastes like a bitter apple that you want the flies to eat,
It looks like bitter cold in the distance,
It smells rotten like maggots crawling on your cuts,
It sounds like nothing, nothing at all just silence,
It reminds me of sad times.

Kitty Marshall (8)
Landscove CE Primary School, Newton Abbot

Laughter

Laughter is joyful like my dad
It feels like I am playing football
It tastes like candyfloss
It looks like white candyfloss
It smells like strawberries
It sounds like an electric guitar
It reminds me of chocolate.

Ashley Stock (8)
Landscove CE Primary School, Newton Abbot

Love

Love is lovely red like a big, red bubbly heart
It feels like a snugly cloud
It tastes like strawberry jam
It looks like a love heart
It smells like roses
It sounds like a hummingbird
It reminds me of being a bride.

Isabelle Luscombe (8)
Landscove CE Primary School, Newton Abbot

Laughter

Laughter is pink like some bubblegum
It feels like the hot sunlight glistening in the air,
It tastes like a lollipop fizzing in your mouth
It looks like a whole pink batch tickling in your stomach.
It smells like the sweet air of the rose
It sounds like a bunch of giggling children
It reminds me of my happy memories.

Yjumye Hurley-Scott (8)
Landscove CE Primary School, Newton Abbot

Fun

Fun is pink like bouncing bunnies,
It feels like you're going round and round on a big fairground wheel.
It tastes like pink marshmallows and fluffy candyfloss,
It looks like big bubbles on a multicoloured rainbow
It smells like chocolate melting in the boiling sun
It sounds like birds singing in the golden morning
It reminds me of the sea on a hot summer's day.

Isabel Hopper (8)
Landscove CE Primary School, Newton Abbot

Anger

Anger is red like a boiling, sizzling oven
It feels like hot frying pans
It tastes like boiling hot sausages
It looks like red-hot flames
It smells like hot steam
It sounds like sizzling
It reminds me of lava.

Barney Latchem (9)
Landscove CE Primary School, Newton Abbot

Laughter

It feels like a feather duster tickling me all the time
It looks like a monkey standing on its head
It tastes like cola fizzing on my tongue
It smells like sugar and spices.
It sounds like children's giggles
It reminds me of yellow.

Freya Christy (8)
Landscove CE Primary School, Newton Abbot

Fun!

Fun is blue like sunny days
It feels like playing with my friends in the park
It tastes like pizza and candyfloss
It looks like spring flavours in the hedgerows
It smells like spring water fresh from a volcano
It sounds like birds singing
It reminds me of my loving family.

Eleanor Biggs (8)
Landscove CE Primary School, Newton Abbot

The Aga

The Aga's hot plates stare at you,
Like frogs' eyes peering out of a murky pond,
Smiling at me with rose red cheeks,
Like Dopey Dan's smile,
Gurgling water in the boiler like a ghost howling,
Open the door,
Whoosh the heat is like a dragon's breath,
Licking round your face.

Nick Hewett (9)
Lifton Community Primary School, Lifton

I Was Going To Write A Poem Today

I was going to write a poem today
But I'm afraid to say I can't
My mind's as empty as a barrel
And every time the faintest trace of an idea appears in my head
It glides like a fish
And slips and slides its way out of my mind
Before I can grab it.

I'm tired of thinking
All through the day
And my brain has gone to bed
He's curled up in a bundle inside my head.

Jonathan Bray (9)
Lifton Community Primary School, Lifton

A Rose Poem

Red, pink and white roses
Standing up straight and still
Petals start to quiver in the gentle summer breeze.
The strawberry coloured rose sparkling in the sun
Rambling roses winding up the tree.
Until *rip* they're pulling away from their roots.

Charlotte Curry (10)
Lifton Community Primary School, Lifton

Teddy Poem

His eyes tiredly stare and stare
As tired Ted falls asleep
His skin is as yellow as a banana
Picked on a hot summer's day,
Tick, tick goes the bean in his belly.

Shannon Hards (10)
Lifton Community Primary School, Lifton

Shelob The Silken Spider

As she spins her bed of silk her eyes glisten like the moon
As the day rises up into the sun she catches a bug or two
And that's her job well done.
She is black like the moonlit sky and has little white dots like stars
As the fly goes fly, fly fly in her web, she injects her poison
                                                    and then the fly dies
She spins silk smoothly around her prey
Now the day goes down into the night she tucks up
Into her silken bed and waits till morning arrives
And starts all over again.

Alice Davies (9)
Lifton Community Primary School, Lifton

Horse Poem

The horses gallop through the night,
In the faint silver moonlight
Heads toss, manes fly
Stars reflect in their eye.

Hooves turn up the soft grass
So silent no one notices as they pass
The horses gallop through the night,
In the faint silver moonlight.

Alice Ricketts (10) & Taila Donnelly (9)
Lifton Community Primary School, Lifton

Fog

He doesn't let anything go past him,
He has a face that crumples if anything tries.
He seems scary but he is magical.
He feels his way around the houses and over things.
He is very dark but he tries to be friendly
His arms wrap around things.

Bethany Lake (9)
Lifton Community Primary School, Lifton

A Poem About Me

The sun is out,
The sky is blue
I go out in the garden
For an hour or two.

I play with my football
Or may have a swing,
I also ride my bike
I do lots of things.

I play by my stream
Then Mum shouts . . .
Ice cream!'
I run indoors and get mud
All over the floor.

It's gone dark and grey
The sun's gone away
No more playing
But I had a
Lovely day!

Christopher Doidge (9)
Lifton Community Primary School, Lifton

Snow

Her flakes are like stars,
As she drips from the sky,
She covers me with a blanket,
As her flakes flutter through the air,
Her white coat covers the ground,
Her white skin reflects the moonlight
She drops her lace powder as she dances,
Her eyes twinkling like frozen water in the sunlight.

Lauren Uzzell (10)
Lifton Community Primary School, Lifton

The Elephant

The elephant stood there in the middle of the jungle,
His great big ears like pillows, stood out among the leaves.
His tusks, strong and mighty shone in the night,
Proud and brave, this elephant we please.
Nothing will frighten this clever elephant, for he is the huge king.
He will crunch away at the bamboo, with his teeth so big.
He'll play with all the animals, small, medium or large,
Or run around breaking all the leaves and twigs.
But, wait, what's that . . . ?
A poacher
'Get off that elephant,' I cry, but the elephant is already dead.

Lydia Gilbert (10)
Lifton Community Primary School, Lifton

Wayne's Wonderful Wacky Pen!

The pen was like a stick with a nib,
It was rosy red as it walked across the book's veins,
Leaving an unplanned route behind him,
Then all of a sudden *bang* the book was slammed shut
                                    and the pen went cuckoo.

Wayne Northam (9)
Lifton Community Primary School, Lifton

Snow

Her eyes twinkle like frozen water in the sunlight,
As she cries vividly.
Her flakes flutter through the air,
As she drips down from the sky.
Her white skin reflects the moonlight,
As her white coat covers the garden.
She covers us with a thick blanket and she drops her dress
                            as she sleeps as if to cover something.

Alice Davies & Tieryn Clark (9)
Lifton Community Primary School, Lifton

Mist

Her pure white cloaks are illusions,
She covers all within her reach gently with her cloaks,
Her cloak covers the rolling hills,
She cuddles the trees only letting the very tips escape,
She creeps through the streets dawn, day noon and night,
She lets not even the crevices of the cliffs escape her white,
Her skin pure as water from fresh springs of the French mountains,
She is as wise as an owl but cheerful as a purring cat,
Her movement is that of a swirling dove in flight,
Swoosh, swoosh as the wind aids her silent travel to her destination,
Gracefully gliding through the air she drapes her cloak along,
Until her skin and cloak both are pierced by a fiery poker
                                        then her illusion is broken.

Daniel Keast (10)
Lifton Community Primary School, Lifton

The Seaside By Night And Day

The shattered moon goes to sleep tiredly
As the yawning sun wakes up.
The whistle of the grass goes to the wind slowly
As the shiny stars makes beautiful pictures
The rock remembers how to play nicely.
So the sea can play with her.

Siobhan Riggs (10)
Lympstone CE Primary School, Lympstone

Another Day Is Done

The shiny sun wakes up after a long sleep.
The moon goes to sleep in his cloudy armchair.
The rock remembers when he was thrown into the water.
The grass whispers when the warm wind blows.

Rebecca Brown (10)
Lympstone CE Primary School, Lympstone

The Dreamy Day

The yawning sun wakes up to the morning dew,
While the birds sing away to their early song.
The clouds reach for their fluffy coats,
Getting ready for their long walk ahead of them,
Chattering, as always, the grasses whisper fades away
                                        to nothing in the breeze.
Weeping till he could cry no more, the bush stands alone in the forest
While the rock, thinking hard about his watery life,
                                was stroking his mossy beard.
The active trees dance away to their midnight song,
And finally the sleepy moon sinks down to his cloudy bed . . .

Jasmine Ousley (10)
Lympstone CE Primary School, Lympstone

A New Day

The round moon rests on the lazy hills,
The golden sun wakes up yawning,
The twinkling stars run away as the sun drifts up.
The crisp grass whispers as the sun appears,
The big rock remembers the beautiful birth of the stars
                                    many years before,
And the bold clouds roll over each other.
A new day is born.

Georgia Goff (10)
Lympstone CE Primary School, Lympstone

Poem Of Your Dreams

The shining stars fly through the air.
The cloud covers the moon as he is off to bed.
The moon goes to sleep.
The sleepy sun wakes from slumber.
The grass is whispering in the gentle wind.

Michael Lockhart (10)
Lympstone CE Primary School, Lympstone

Another Day Is Done

The moon goes to sleep in his warm cloudy bed
As the sun wakes up after a good night's sleep,
The stars twinkle as they go down,
And the dawn dreams of the day ahead.
The rock remembers his old crusty life,
And the sea dances over the sand,
The shiny sun goes to sleep,
And the moon and stars come up,
The grass whispers as the north wind blows,
And another day is done.

Kelsey Clayton (11)
Lympstone CE Primary School, Lympstone

The Living Night

The grass is whispering to his friend the north wind.
The stars shine bright like a light.
The moon goes to sleep on a cloudy bed.
And the rock and the pebbles whisper to echo.

Jack Gardner (10)
Lympstone CE Primary School, Lympstone

Summer Days

The hot sun wakes
And burns on the blue horizon,
And the birds begin to sing
In the whistling trees.
Then the ancient rocks
Remember all.
The grass begins to whisper
In the wild winds.
This is the end.
The stars sparkle like glitter on paper
And the moon goes to sleep.

Carla Griffin (10)
Lympstone CE Primary School, Lympstone

The Journey Of Night

The sparkling sun dances as it goes down,
The sea dreams while crashing against the sand,
The dawn dances on the horizon.

The moon looks down on the Earth,
The night dances, as all the clocks strike midnight,
The twinkling stars shine brightly at night,
The moonlight dances on the water
The stars bring memories.

Lauren Mingo (10)
Lympstone CE Primary School, Lympstone

Night/Day

The moonlight dances on the water.
And the stars guide us.
The Earth is being protected by the sky
The night makes us sleep and tucks us into bed.

While brightening the Earth, the sun wakes up.
And the moon fades away behind the misty mountains.
The grass begins to whisper.
The Earth has been transformed from night to day.

Behn Wright (10)
Lympstone CE Primary School, Lympstone

The Night Looks Upon Us

The stars twinkle as they dance.
The moon brings light in the middle of the night.
The sea smashes against the rocks.
The stars bring happy memories.
The night dances as the clock strikes.

Sophie Morgan (10)
Lympstone CE Primary School, Lympstone

The Slumbering Sun

The shiny sun wakes up from slumber.
The moon goes to sleep behind dark misty mountains.
The sweet grasses whistle while the west wind blows.
The birds sing.

Jack Amphlett (10)
Lympstone CE Primary School, Lympstone

Autumn Time Is Here

Autumn time is here
Hedgehogs fear,
Wind chimes *clonk*
Conkers k'donk.

Autumn time is here
The sky is clear
The wind blows through the trees
Making a very nasty breeze.

Autumn time is here
Wind is on the way so cover up your ears.
Red rust, yellow, brown
Leaves scattered on the ground.

Autumn time has gone
People coming too and from,
Do not fear
Cos wintertime is here.

Gabby Reynolds & Clovie Knight (10)
Marhamchurch Primary School, Bude

Autumn!

The autumn leaves
Fall with the breeze
A sudden colour of
Yellow, red and green.

Rusty browns fall
To the ground along with
Browny reds and
Golden yellows.

The thud of an apple
Sounds all around
An occasional
Squelchy sound.

Spiky shells
On the ground
Inside is a shiny brown
Conker!

Louise Kerr (10)
Marhamchurch Primary School, Bude

My Hobbies

I love music
I love sport
I love history
English? Not!

The sound of music in the street,
Everybody's rocking to the beat,
Scoring and saving the football kings,
They look around while the loud crowd rings,
Oh and if you are an Egyptian mummy,
You won't mind me saying you look funny.

Anna Newman (9)
Moretonhampstead Primary School, Newton Abbot

The Blank Page

For our English lesson all this week,
We have to write a poem.
A poem about mice and cats, dogs and rats.
Rabbits and ravens, bugs and beetles,
At first I thought it would be easy
Easy-peasy lemon squeezy
I had an idea then I lost it
Oh what a blow
How could I sink so low?
I tap my pen on the paper
What could I do?
What could I do?
My friends are doing all OK
But here I am still sitting here
But with one big difference
I have an *idea!*

Sarah Stewart-Watson (9)
Moretonhampstead Primary School, Newton Abbot

The Knight

Imagine a silver suit placed upon a man
Striding on a ghost-white horse,
To save people throughout the land,
Slaying fierce fire-breathing dragons,
To save pretty princesses from high towers,
Killing all evil things,
This wonderful man has all the power,
But one thing that we don't know
Who he is and where he goes,
He is a knight in shining armour,
And all the rest I don't know.

Caroline Francis (10)
Moretonhampstead Primary School, Newton Abbot

Dragons And Wizards

D ragons are fiery, frightening and ferocious
R ude and mysterious
A ngry and
G o
O n riots, rampages and make lots of
N oise,
S melling like old smelly Wellington boots.

A ngry and
N ice,
D isasters are all covered in jelly.

W izards look angry but are sometimes nice,
I ndividual wizards have individual spells,
Z apping enemies into space,
A ccidents happening,
R ound the house,
D isasters all happening every hour with
S uccess and completing their goal.

Sam Goodwyn (10)
Moretonhampstead Primary School, Newton Abbot

Animals

L is for lazy yellow lion, sleeping in the hot sunny jungle
O is for chocolate brown otter, playing on the dry grassy bank.
R is for creamy grey rhino, on the dry sandy desert.
I is for insects on the light brown tree, eating away
                                    some lovely leaves
N is for newt all soggy in a dirty pond, swimming
                                    around very happily
E is for elephant all nice and *fat* stamping around
                        If you go under me you're nothing but *flat!*

Lorine Parkinson (10)
Moretonhampstead Primary School, Newton Abbot

The Chaos Family

I live in the chaos family
My dad is pulling his hair out
My mum is ironing the bacon,
My baby sister is screaming really loud,
My puppies are chewing all of our shoes
My best friend is arguing with me
My twin brothers are messing up the house.
My older brother is playing the drums,
My cousin is putting bugs up his nose,
My family is *chaos!*

Hollie Brackenbury (10)
Moretonhampstead Primary School, Newton Abbot

Ancient Egypt

I am a mean mummy, mean as can be.
I am a pointed pyramid, pointed as can be.
I am a crafted tomb, good as can be.
I am a great pharaoh, great as can be.
I am a clean slave, clean as can be.
I am a scarab beetle, pretty as can be,
I am the town as lovely as can be.

Rebekah Austin (9)
Moretonhampstead Primary School, Newton Abbot

Quick 007

Sneak around the building,
Go in the door,
And go spy on Sam X,
He escapes on an airplane and he lands on a military aircraft carrier
He gets on a super boat,
And I'm still chasing him!

Tommy Newell (9)
Moretonhampstead Primary School, Newton Abbot

What Do I Love?

I love football,
I love rugby,
I love cricket,
But I don't love you,
I love tennis,
I love basketball
I love netball,
But I still don't love you.
I love my mum
I love my dad,
I love my brother,
But just take it I don't love you.

Joe Colridge (9)
Moretonhampstead Primary School, Newton Abbot

Labradors

Labradors like to breathe fire
Labradors like to play with bones that are balls,
Labradors like to bite you,
Labradors like to snap at bumblebees
Labradors like to walk on two legs,
Labradors like to wag their tails.

Hannah Austin (9)
Moretonhampstead Primary School, Newton Abbot

What Am I?

I am big and round, what am I?
I am white and cold, what am I?
I am the king of winter, what am I?
I am handmade by people, what am I?
I am a thing with a vegetable nose, what am I?
What am I? I am a snowman!

Cara Bell (10)
Moretonhampstead Primary School, Newton Abbot

Magic Months Of The Year!

Joyful, jealous, January
Funny, fantastic, February
Mad, magnificent, March.
Amazing, annoying, April
Magnetic, marvellous, May.
Jazzy, jiggy, June.
Jumbly, Japanese, July.
Aggressive, anxious, August
Showjumping, sensible, September
Offensive, oozy, October
Naughty, noisy, November
Dizzy, daydreaming, December.
Magic months of the year!

Hannah Goodwin (9)
Moretonhampstead Primary School, Newton Abbot

I'm A Funny Bunny

I'm a funny bunny
I'm a blue bird,
I'm a cook's book,
I'm a cat herd.

I'm an iron lion
I'm a dirty football,
I'm a mud floor,
I'm a wood door.

I'm a funny bunny.

Teresa Hellyer (9)
Moretonhampstead Primary School, Newton Abbot

The Stables

T he horses are tired,
H ay they do eat,
E ating is favourite, they all fall asleep,

S traw, they have bedding,
T eeth, they have blunt,
A nd all have to work and jump,
B ending is hard but you go very fast,
L earning is hard and you do get to play,
E ating their feed as they gobble it up,
S leeping in stable, all curled up.

See you in morning, do wake *up*.

Lisa Tribe (10)
Moretonhampstead Primary School, Newton Abbot

Kimberley

K is for kangaroo jumping in the desert
I   is for insect scuttling across a log
M is for mouse nibbling the cheese
B is for birdsong in the trees
E is for eagle flying in the trees
R is for rabbit hopping in the run
L is for lion roaring through the trees
E is for elephant stomping through the trees.
Y is for yellow bird bright as the sun.

Kimberley Thomas (10)
Moretonhampstead Primary School, Newton Abbot

Trial Bikes

T rial bikes jumping rock to rock
R ocky rocks making stages hard
I cy rocks making bikes slip
A mazing tricks done on giant dirt jumps
L eaping bikes flying in the air and over me.

B ikes racing down through the woods
I cy hills icy grounds lookout bikes about
K ing-size rocks that bikes can jump
E xcellent bikes doing amazing tricks
S lippy wheels slipping on rocks in the stage.

Alex Amery (10)
Moretonhampstead Primary School, Newton Abbot

My Guitar

Supersonic sounding guitar?
    Calling a song out from a bar!
        Amplifying an amazing anonymous sound!
        Ruling the world of rock!

Letting a loose sound of music tunnel around your head!
    Excellent outstanding music played from my guitar?
        Telling a tale about the cost of your guitar!
        Tasks telling you to take a step forward!

Scarlett Garland (10)
Moretonhampstead Primary School, Newton Abbot

The Animal Kingdom

One day in the wild wacky jungle . . .
10 parrots prancing prettily pictured on pines,
9 monkeys making mischievous mayhem madly,
8 snakes slithering on slimy sluggish sand,
7 lizards looping lively like lean leopards
6 ants annoying athletic awesome antelopes,
5 spiders spinning silky spirals while singing songs
4 giraffes jumping jazzy jackpots,
3 elephants electing easy elements for exercise,
2 centipedes sliding softly along salty salads.
Last but not least the *lion!*

Charlotte Farrer (10)
Moretonhampstead Primary School, Newton Abbot

Motocross

M agnificent speed around the track,
O bservant and wanting to win,
T ackling the jumps big or small,
O bedient and skilful,
C atching and overtaking
R acing round and round, up and down,
O h no he has fallen off, along comes an ambulance to pick him up
S uper - place 1st it is
S tart of the next season, willing for first again.

Harry Hampton (10)
Moretonhampstead Primary School, Newton Abbot

Our Class

Our walls are as white as a rubber
Our tables are as brown as wood,
Our pupils have jumpers as blue as the sea,
My pencil case is as jazzy as a disco,
Our teacher has tiny tables and
Our class does silly science
Our class does easy English
Our class does groovy geography
Our class does musical maths
Our class does adding art,
Our class does mad music,
We do plastic PE and
We have girly girls and silly boys
What a wonderful class!

Iesha Chaney (8)
St Mellion CE Primary School, Saltash

Our Class

Red books, blue rules,
Old teachers, new pupils,
Boys that are silly,
Girls that are pretty,
Shirts that are white,
Shoes that are black,
Books that are orange
Books that are green,
Old tables, new chairs,
New rubbers, old pencils.

Holly Hemmens (8)
St Mellion CE Primary School, Saltash

Clowns

Bright clowns,
Dull clowns,
Old clowns,
New clowns,
Clowns that are funny,
Clowns that are dumb,
Clowns that go right,
Clowns that go wrong,
Hairy clowns
Bold clowns,
Clowns that are big,
Clowns that are small,
Clowns that are fast,
Clowns that are slow,
Wicked clowns,
Weird clowns.
I love clowns.

Luke Hewison (8)
St Mellion CE Primary School, Saltash

Games

Fun games
Boring games
Small games
Big games
Slow games
Fast games
Red games
Blue games
Tiny games
Large games
Old games
New games
I love games.

Ben Jeffery (7)
St Mellion CE Primary School, Saltash

Football

Educated England
Booting Beckham is bending those balls
Amazing Alan Smith is acting acrobats
Octopus Owen is outstanding.

Magnificent Man U
Racing Rooney is running around Reaves!
Running Ronaldo is racing rapidly
Hopping Howard is home sweet home.

At lazy Liverpool
Sissy Cissa is silly
Batting Baros is boring
Dummy Dueduck is dumb.

Chatting Chelsea
Limping Lampard is loopy
Tearing Terry is tackling
Catching Czech isn't cool.

Appalling Arsenal
Hairy Henry is hairy
Guilty Gillberto is going
Leaping Leaman is lean.

Joseph Grocott (8)
St Mellion CE Primary School, Saltash

Our Classroom

I saw a funny classroom
With a funny teacher
With a funny lesson
We have funny fun
Then comes funny lunch
After funny lunch
We have funny PE
Then go we go funny home.

Dominick Chiswell (8)
St Mellion CE Primary School, Saltash

Our Classroom

In our classroom
Alongside the door,
There are some pegs and many more,
In the reading corner we have got many books,
Quite a lot,
Under the table you can see
Very clean and shiny feet!
On the table you can see
A very happy and cheerful me,
Next to the sink you can see
A large tray of drinks for you and me.
Over the computers you can see
A great display of the Caribbean sea
If you go to the desk you can meet
Miss Welch, the best.
Down behind the kitchen doors
A lovely cook lay in store.

Rhianna Darby (9)
St Mellion CE Primary School, Saltash

Horses

Brown horses that look like chocolate
White horses that look like snow,
Black horses that are as black as coal,
Old horses that look like my grandad,
New horses that are jump and jolly
Horses that are shy like the sun tucking away ready for another day
Horses with saddles on them
Horses without
Horses with reins,
Fast horses that run like the wind
Slow horses that are as slow as a snail
Horses are fantastic and fun!

Amelia Fox (9)
St Mellion CE Primary School, Saltash

Funny Goldfish

I saw a funny goldfish in a funny bowl,
He said to me in a funny sort of way,
'Please do go away you're in the light,
You're not a very pretty sight'
I moved away
I didn't want to stay.
I stopped and stared for a while, he gave me a funny sort of smile
'Why are you staring at me?' he said
I looked away and said
'You're a strange and funny goldfish who should have food'
'I want my tea,' he replied
So I gave him a can of food nice and dried
He smiled and said, 'Thanks a lot
But next time make it sooner you silly clot.'

Sophie Northcott (9)
St Mellion CE Primary School, Saltash

The Simpsons

Oh, The Simpsons, it's really, really good
You see Homer Simpson eating doughnuts as his pud.
Not to forget shopkeeper Apu,
He's got a whole store of doughnuts for you!
You can't forget Lisa,
She plays the saxophone,
Although it may sound a bit like a drone.
Let's not forget to mention Bart,
Without him the show would fall apart.
And then there's Mr Burns,
Once got shot,
So Maggie got three years, locked in her cot.

This poem was written by Chris,
As The Simpsons is a programme not to be missed.

Christopher Dwane (9)
St Mellion CE Primary School, Saltash

Football Teams

Red teams, blue teams
Old teams, new teams
Teams that are good
Teams that are bad
Teams that do lose
Teams that are tight
Teams that are fast
Teams with might
Teams that are green
And cheat you teams
Teams that are yellow
Teams that are white
Teams that are dirty
Teams that are clean
Teams for great matches
Teams for cool players
My team will win!

Dean Lambert (9)
St Mellion CE Primary School, Saltash

Computer

White computer
Grey monitors
Yellow lights as bright as stars
Old one new ones
Computers are fast like machines
Computers that load as fast as bullets
Computers bright as sunset
Computers with games are groovy and great
Computers are crazy fun!

Liam Maton (9)
St Mellion CE Primary School, Saltash

Doggerel

This poem will continue for a dog's age,
And it is a bit of a personal dogma
I looked up at the amazing dog-star and sat in admiration,
I've been called a dog in a manger many times before,
They say I've been dogging them but there a bore.

I never could have had a dog's life,
But when I came to any dog's leg
I turned the wrong way,
I saw hundreds of dogfish, which had gone to the dogs
                                            and in my kennel I lay
They have been dogging me for ages I had been aware
                    of their scary dogfight when they stop and stare.
Each held up a dog rose
Now I am a dog rose,
So I jump with glee - because finally I am happy.

Ben Farrar (11)
St Mellion CE Primary School, Saltash

Doggeral

This story is as long as a dog's age,
And I like being dogmatic,
I looked up at the amazing dog-star and felt like a fanatic,
I'm not a god in the manger,
I was dogging like a bloodhound.

I went through cities having dogfights,
Going round dogs' ears and dogs' legs all the time,
But now I am a dog rose, all that dog-eat-dog is gone!
You could say I am dogmatic
But you'd be very wrong.

Dan Ball (10)
St Mellion CE Primary School, Saltash

On Our Pirate Ship

On our pirate ship we have got . . .
Two plump parrots
Three sharp sounds
Four crazy crewmates
Five plum-shaped prisoners
Six super shot cannons
Seven dangerous daggers
Eight crumpled cabin crew
Nine dopey dogs
Ten shuffling skeletons
And
One clumsy captain.

Alex Jeffery (9)
St Mellion CE Primary School, Saltash

Drum Set

Loud drums,
Quiet drums,
Old drums,
New drums,
Flat drums,
Tall drums,
Big drums,
Small drums
Bass drum
Snare drums
Old cymbals,
New cymbals,
I love drums.

Tim Page (10)
St Mellion CE Primary School, Saltash

Skaters And Teams

Excellent, expensive element,
Anywhere goes amazing Adio,
Hunting happy hawk,
Ponging poison public,
Put a pin in planet Earth
Riding rhino
Skater's at birth,
Tumbling Tony Hawk,
Bouncing Bam Margera,
Chanting Chad Muskay
Not excellent Ellissa Steamer
Get me a deck I love to skate, I'll get more mates
I promise I won't be home too late.

Joshua Paul (10)
St Mellion CE Primary School, Saltash

Doggeral

This may go on for a dog's age
But this is my dogma
I looked at the amazing dog-star and sat in deep thought
People say I'm a dog in a manger but they are being dogmatic.
I feel like someone is dogging me like a spy in the war, it's dramatic.

Sometimes I feel like I'm leading a dog's life
But surely it should be a dog's dinner not all this strife.
I'm a dogfighter not a dog rose!
I'm dogged and ruthless like a dogfish
Am I dogmatic? You wish.

Tom Ransome (10)
St Mellion CE Primary School, Saltash

Tranquillity In The Waves

Calm and peaceful,
   Quiet and still
      The sea: in the power and greatness,
         As smooth as a cat's warm fur.

      Under its surface,
   Below the waves,
The sea: in its splendour and beauty,
Hidden from life on the land.

Darting fast, yet
   Sleek and graceful.
      The sea: with its shimmering dolphins,
         Happy and joyful they play.

      Lapping the islands,
   Splashing the beach.
The sea will never stop moving,
Its tides working day and night.

Alex Everett (10)
Sampford Peverell CE Primary School, Tiverton

Hidie

I am a young goat called Hidie
I have a owner called Maggie
Between us we have lots of fun.
We dance and skip together,
We talk and sing together,
When it comes to bedtime
We eat chocolate ice cream and apples
And say goodnight.

Margaret Palmer (9)
Sampford Peverell CE Primary School, Tiverton

The Sun, Moon And Rainbow Time

Stars shine at misty moonlight,
The sun comes round,
The moon mysteriously
Rotates and disappears,
Through the clear daylight
Like a magnifying glass,
Shining at day.

The moon sparkling
At night,
Like a torch
Down a dark gloomy pipe
Nocturnal animals
Creeping at night
And sleeping at day.

Planets fade
At bright daylight
You and I
See the moon
Raising and fading
Like eating a lolly.
And it disappears,
Into our throats.

Rainbows come,
Then rest,
For the crest,
The sun shines
And the moon,
Gets ready to rise
The moon, the sun and rainbow.

All fade at different times,
Everyone needs,
Rest and to be awake
For times,
Go flying past
At different times,
Of day and night.

Samuel Kendall (8)
Tregony Primary School, Tregony

Midnight Murder

It's silent apart from . . .
Tiptoe . . .
    Tiptoe . . .
        Tiptoe . . .
Uh oh! It's coming up the corridor
Bubble-bubble I can't believe it's happening
My brother is a-burning!

Crunch-crunch bones being stamped on!
I pull up the cover but the sides won't tuck in

They open my door, I feel their breath
It's midnight murder, they're dedicated to death!
They're opening my door and say . . .
'Darling do you want a cup of tea, looks like you've seen a ghost!'

Zoe Waters (8)
Tregony Primary School, Tregony

The Giraffe

The graceful giraffe,
Eyes beautiful as sparkly stars shining
Bright in the light.

Fur brown and yellow
Like a princess
She's the star of the show.

The land love's her creatures
She's the queen of the world
The pop Party.

So nobody she meet's is as beautiful.

Lauren Shearing (9)
Tregony Primary School, Tregony

The Moon

The moon is cheese
The stars are bright
The sun is hot
The sun is yellow
The stars are a twinkle
The moon is round
The sunset is colourful
The sunset is different colours
Like orange red and all sorts
The Earth is round
The Earth moves
The clouds are candy.

Conor Pearce (8)
Tregony Primary School, Tregony

My Mum's Pony

My mum's pony had some yummy food,
My mum's pony had a ride to the beach,
My mum's pony saw a friend at the beach,
My mum's pony has a girlfriend
My mum's pony has suncream
My mum's pony is shy
I love my mum's pony.

Georgie Green (7)
Tregony Primary School, Tregony

Love

Love feels like happiness
Love feels like your heart is thumping
Love is the colour of red,
Love feels heart-shaped
Love is marriage.

Chris Thomas (9)
Tregony Primary School, Tregony

Eagles, Eggs

Eagles, earphones
Eagles, earthquakes
Eagles, earthworm.

Eagles, eighteen
Eagles, Egyptians
Eagles, ego

Eagles, elves
Eagles, escape
Eagles, embrace

Eagles, earthly
Eagles, Easter
Eagles, eggplant

Eagles, exceeded
Eagles, except
Eagles, exude.

Brannon Cummins (8)
Tregony Primary School, Tregony

The Jungle

Tigers, tigers leaping light,
When will you come out tonight?

Monkeys, monkeys swing so bright,
When will you come out tonight?

Spiders, spiders creeping so right
When will you come out tonight?

The lions for a fight
So come tonight

The monkeys are coming
So are the spiders
And the tigers.

So we will win for sure!

Chloe Ringrose (9)
Tregony Primary School, Tregony

The Moon

The moon is made of cheese
The clouds are made of candyfloss
Stars are made of sugar
Earth is made of a boiled sweet.

And Mars is made of fudge
The rain is fizzy pop
Pluto is made of a blueberry
The hail is ice cream
And the soil is made of chocolate.

But is the moon really made of cheese?

Robert Wilshaw (8)
Tregony Primary School, Tregony

Getting A Dog

White dogs, black dogs, brown dogs too,
Freckled faces and a wet nose,
Kennels fresh as new.

Big dogs, fat dogs, small too
Wagging tails, soft paws, cheeky smiles,
Lots of dog walking!

Elowen Gray-Roberts (7)
Tregony Primary School, Tregony

Black Rider

He'll ride at night not day,
His tattered horse, Black Mane,
He rides at night from his deadly face
His feathered hat rages out,
The sun comes up and he disappears . . .
Disappears . . . disappears . . . disappears . . . disappears . . .

Amanda Butfield (9)
Tregony Primary School, Tregony

The Moon

The moon is made of cheese
The stars are made of biscuits
The sun is made of Sunny D
And the Earth is made of liquorish.

The rickety ragged road is made of chocolate
The animals are made of Haribos
And the shops are made of grass
Shining glittering grass.

Curtis Cowl (8)
Tregony Primary School, Tregony

Cats

Fluffy cats, rough cats
Wet noses, dry noses,
White cats, black cats,
All types of cats on the street.

Bad cats, good cats,
Scratchy cats, clean cats,
Brown cats, ginger cats
All types of cats on the street.

Sophie Jackson (8)
Tregony Primary School, Tregony

The Zoo

Silly monkeys
Frustrated rhinos,
Fierce lions,
Noisy tigers,
Slithering snakes,
Snapping crocodiles,
I love the zoo.

Jacob Bunney (7)
Tregony Primary School, Tregony

Spooky Spider

Spooky spider creeping up the hall,
Coming to get you all.

As black as a shadow,
As black as a hole,
Legs as long as a purple pole.

Sneaky spider creeping up the hall,
Sly, sneaky, coming to get you all.

As black as a shadow
As black as a hole,
Legs as long as a purple pole.

Eleanor Wood (8)
Tregony Primary School, Tregony

The Circus

I saw dangerous tricks,
I saw girls dancing,
I saw ladies singing,
I saw a party,
I heard music,
I heard a baby crying
I had a great time.

Nichola Goldworthy (8)
Tregony Primary School, Tregony

The Beach

Seagulls screeching,
Big boats passing,
Children playing in the sea,
People flying kites,
Sandcastle making,
Another day at the beach!

Ysabelle Smith (7)
Tregony Primary School, Tregony

Funny Planets And Stuff In Space

The hail is made of Haribos
The moon is made of cheddar cheese
The meteors are made of stone crystals
And the rain is fizzy pop.

Mars is made of gob stoppers
Pluto is made of jellybeans
But the strange one is Saturn which is made of stones.

And the last one is smarty space,
And I almost forgot . . .
The Milky Way.

Sean Gibson (8)
Tregony Primary School, Tregony

The Beach

Golden soft sand
Sea shining like a gold coin
Sky was as blue as can be,
Children playing with the sand and sea,
Parents sleeping and resting,
Seagulls dipping into the sea for fish,
Crabs crawling across the sand.

Jack Emery (8)
Tregony Primary School, Tregony

The Moon

Moon, moon, glorious moon gliding across the bright blue sky.
Moon, moon, shining brightly across the sky reflections
                                                    on the ocean blue.
Moon, moon, glorious moon I think you're made of cheese . . .
Moon, moon, your craters are like bomb holes from the war.

Nathan Cowl (9)
Tregony Primary School, Tregony

What's My Animal?

Thick black stripes,
Fluffy orange fur,
Big sharp teeth,
Very fierce,
Eats meat,
Very scary,
In a jungle,
It's a . . .
Tiger!

Rachael O'Brien (8)
Tregony Primary School, Tregony

I Saw An Animal

I saw an eagle with rocket launchers,
That fire out flaming fireballs,
It had an army man's hat,
And a golden, bright beak,
It had a bazooka on each wing,
And rocket boosters for a tail
It was the size of an elephant,
And flew as fast as a Concorde.

Andrew Barton (7)
Tregony Primary School, Tregony

Farm

Cows making fresh milk,
Tractors ploughing rows,
Pigs running around like maniacs,
Sheep eating fresh grass,
Horses in a warm stable.

Michael Berridge (8)
Tregony Primary School, Tregony

My Horse

White soft hair,
Big strong hooves,
Long elegant nose,
Smooth small ears,
Thin silky back,
Glossy grey tail,
Sparkly shiny eyes
My horse is special.

Bethany Grant (7)
Tregony Primary School, Tregony

The Hospital

People chatting
Trolleys squeaking,
Buzzers buzzing,
Nurses scurrying,
Doors banging,
Lifts moving,
Patients talking,
Doctors shouting.

Thomas Oatey (7)
Tregony Primary School, Tregony

Star Shine

Star shine in the night
With the glow they guide your sight
Stars are golden
Stars are bright,
They guide your night . . .
In use of bright.

Elizabeth Oatey (8)
Tregony Primary School, Tregony

I Have A Tiger In My Room

I opened the door,
And got such a fright,
It was a tiger!
It was an amazing sight.

It was 8 foot tall,
With sharp white claws,
He had dark vivid stripes,
And saucer like paws.

The tiger didn't hurt me,
He was really kind and nice,
I tried to feed him meat,
But he would only eat rice.

I cried to my mum 'There's a tiger in my room,'
My mum went to have a look,
But all she would say was . . .
'You must have got your imagination from a book.'

I have a tiger in my cupboard,
Nobody can see him but me,
We are very happy together,
My tiger and me.

Claire Thompson (10)
Troon Primary School, Camborne

Kids Say Thing's Like . . .

I don't want to play with you because I am playing with someone else
Do you want to skip?
Do you want to play ball?
Do you want some pizza?
Don't push in the line,
Don't lean on me please.

Amber Wise (10)
Troon Primary School, Camborne

Parents Say Things Like . . .

Parents say things like . . .
Tidy up your room,
Why are you making such a loud boom?
Stop fiddling with your hair,
We could go to the hairdressers over there?
We're going out now
Why are you acting like a cow?
Cry as much as you want
Tell your dad to change that font
There's no such word as can't (well cannot then)
Don't chant
Don't shout
Or you'll get a clout
Sit up,
Or you'll break that cup.

Can't we make our own decisions?
Don't do this and don't do that.

Amber Mankee (10)
Troon Primary School, Camborne

Teachers Say Things Like . . .

Teachers say things like . . .
Don't do that
Sit up
Come on
Do your work
Stop messing around
Sit on the carpet
Be quiet
Stop playing with her hair
Tidy up
Don't drink when I am talking.

Liam Kevern (11)
Troon Primary School, Camborne

Teachers And Children Say Things Like . . .

Teachers and children always say things like . . .
Homework,
Oh Miss,
Get on with your work,
But I am,
Sit up,
Oh Miss it hurts my back,
Take off that hat,
OK I will,
Don't drink while I'm talking,
Oh Miss I'm thirsty,
On the carpet now,
Oh Miss do we have to?
Dinnertime
Yes finally,
Stop fiddling on the carpet,
OK Miss I will and I'm bored.
Home time everyone,
Yes, yes, yes, yes.

Paige Bennett (10)
Troon Primary School, Camborne

The Writer Of This Poem

(Based on 'The writer of this Poem' by Roger McGough)

The writer of this poem
Is as long as a twig
As white as a ghost,
As fluffy as a wig.

As lovely as a flower,
As quick as a lick,
As strong as a boulder,
As straight as a stick.

Yasmin Baker (10)
Troon Primary School, Camborne

The Writer Of This Poem

(Based on 'The Writer of this Poem' by Roger McGough)

The writer of this poem . . .
Is as cuddly as a bear,
As strong as a tree,
As bouncy as a hare,
As smooth as a pen,
As cold as a pole,
As tasty as a sweet
As deep as a hole.

As tall as a sky skyscraper,
As spiky as a holly bush,
As watery as an ocean,
As quiet as a ssh,
As bold as a boxing glove,
As lanky as a thin twig,
As rude as a lion,
As lovely as a wig.

Liam Spear (10)
Troon Primary School, Camborne

Do This, Do That . . .

Teachers say things like . . .
Don't play with your hair,
Don't swing on your chair,
Don't play truth or dare.

Teachers say things like . . .
Do your homework now!
Don't have a row,
Always do a bow.

Bradley Mills (10)
Troon Primary School, Camborne

The Hideous Hovel

Climb the wall and you will find
Biting brambles that gnaw your behind.

Tunnel through the jungle of weeds,
The vines and the roots like electric leads.

Trees tower much too tall,
Never to die, and never to fall.

Find the window, where is the glass?
Clamber in and leave the lofty grass.

Examine the prison, all musty and old,
The smell was unwelcoming, the feeling cold.

Enter a room and you will discover,
A red velvet sofa with a muddy cover.

This is a haven for the weird and the poor,
With it's broken glass windows and boarded up door.

Daniel Buckingham (10)
Troon Primary School, Camborne

Every Day

Every day,
I'm thinking of you,
I wish I didn't let you go,
I want you here with me,
Flying kites in the breeze.

Every day,
I've never stopped loving you,
I close my eyes and you're here,
I'm counting the days we've been apart,
I wish you were here with me.

Ebony Ellis (10)
Troon Primary School, Camborne

Grown-Ups Say Things Like

Grown-ups say things like . . .
Go outside and play with your friends,
Don't go outside because you're grounded,
Go and tidy your room,
Go and stop him now,
Go and grab him,
Eat your breakfast now.

Zack Cooper (10)
Troon Primary School, Camborne

Nurses Say Things Like . . .

Don't get out of bed,
Shall I bandage your head?
Let's go and have a wash,
Time for some squash,
It's time for an operation,
Don't worry it's only a bit of co-operation,
Have you eaten your beef?
Time to clean your teeth.

Bethany Gould (11)
Troon Primary School, Camborne

A Wolf In Me

I have a wolf in me,
Sprinting quietly,
Loudly howling,
Fiercely growling,
Pouncing playfully,
People don't come to me,
I hide away in my den.

Aimee Mayhew Brokenshire (10)
Troon Primary School, Camborne

The Writer Of This Poem

(Based on 'The Writer of This Poem' by Roger McGough)

The writer of this poem . . .
Is as strong as a bear,
As sweet as a flower,
As bouncy as a hare.

As fierce as a lion,
As tall as a tree,
As tasty as an ice cream,
As buzzy as a bee.

As spiky as a hedgehog
As smelly as a pig,
As happy as a swan,
As thin as a twig.

Amy Andrew (10)
Troon Primary School, Camborne

Teachers Say Things Like . . .

Sit down
Be quiet
Stop playing with her hair
Sit up
Be quiet
Do your work
Stop fiddling
Sit up
Stop messing around
Tidy up.

David Wills (10)
Troon Primary School, Camborne

Sea-Bear

In the waves he tumbles and barks,
He trips and tiptoes among the sharks.
He dances among the seaweed,
In the rocks at great speed.

He growls at all the seahorses,
He crushes all the sand houses.
In the shadows he lurks ready to strike,
Watching all the fish and pike.

He comes to shore as a man
To feast on all the cockles in a fan.
Then he slips back in like a crab,
Then gets a sea cab.

Madeleine Moore (10)
Troon Primary School, Camborne

Bossing Around

Police say things like . . .
Stop, you're under arrest,
Stop fighting,
Get out of the car and put your hands up
Excuse me mam have you seen this man?
'Ello, 'ello, 'ello, who's this then?
Stop, police
Now you can get out of jail
Are you OK?
Go, go, go.

Caine Hocking (10)
Troon Primary School, Camborne

I See A Horse

I see a horse racing the Grand National
Like a bullet out of a gun.
I see a horse showjumping
Like a kangaroo jumping across the plain.
I see a horse shaking its skin like a person shivering,
I see a horse swishing its tail windscreen wiper style,
I see a horse pooing like apples falling from an apple tree.

Lauren Saunders (8)
Two Moors Primary School, Tiverton

I See A Puppy

It wags its tail like a hand waving
It is as small as a toilet roll
He chews his bone like a piece of chewing gum
He is as fast as a motorbike on a racetrack.
He pants like a heart beating
Its fur is as soft as cotton wool.

Harriot Taylor (8)
Two Moors Primary School, Tiverton

Rat

Long tail-follower
Wine-sipper
Tea-taker
Beer-nicker
Leftover-eater
Self-washer
Chair-scratcher
Cage-climber
Nose-sniffer.

Caitlin Owen (8)
Two Moors Primary School, Tiverton

Hamster Kennings

Poo-dropper
Exercise-sprinter
Food-eater
Fast-sleeper
Noise-maker
Fast-jogger
Water-drinker
Nasty-biter
Mess-maker
Ear-listener
Eye-spotter.

Mikesh Mistry (8)
Two Moors Primary School, Tiverton

A Horse

Stable dweller
Showjumper
Fly attracter
Apple eater
Bad kicker
Apple pooer.

Megan Buckingham (8)
Two Moors Primary School, Tiverton

A Horse

Carrot-nicker
Apple-cruncher
Muzzle-user
Bad-bucker
Polo-smeller
Apple-plopper.

Cody Norwell (9)
Two Moors Primary School, Tiverton

Cat

Bed-nicker
Floor-wrecker
Tail-swisher
Fur ball-maker
Leg-licker
Food-begger
Face-scratcher
Lap-leaper
Greedy-eater
Smell-maker.

Emily Payne (8)
Two Moors Primary School, Tiverton

Armadillo

Rolling-sprinter
Egg-nicker
Reptile-eater
No noise-maker
Tail-curler
Nose-sniffer
Fat-eater.

Kieron Chard-Maple (8)
Two Moors Primary School, Tiverton

Cat

Eye-shiner
Lap-nicker
Bed-nicker
Slow worm-eater
Mouse-hunter
Tail-wagger
Bird-catcher.

Jessica Willis (9)
Two Moors Primary School, Tiverton

A Hamster

Finger-biter
Food-muncher
Wheel-runner
Fur-licker
Bar-climber
Water-drinker
Long-sleeper
Quick-jumper
I see a hamster drinking his water like a hippo sucking up the lake
He licks his fur like washing the windows of a car
He climbs bars very high like a really fast leaper,
He runs in his wheel it's like a running machine,
He bites fingers like pins being dug into you.
He munches his food quite loudly,
It's like crunching on an onion ring.

Jake Ware (8)
Two Moors Primary School, Tiverton

I See A Cat

Fat-sleeper
Wide-walker
Food-beggar
Lap-jumper
Scratch-maker
Bed-nicker
Tail-twitcher
Eye-shiner
Fur-smoother
Mouth-purrer
Bird-catcher
Paper-ripper
Mouse-eater.

Jessica Payne (8)
Two Moors Primary School, Tiverton

A Horse

Grass muncher
Tail swisher
Bad bucker
Stable dweller
Showjumper
Polo eater

I see a horse . . .
Its tail swishes like a snake slithering
It poos like apples falling from a tree.
Its skin is as silk as the sand.
It gallops like lightning in a storm.
And it jumps over jumps like a kangaroo.

Alisha Gooding (8)
Two Moors Primary School, Tiverton

Horse Kennings

Apple-nicker
Grass-muncher
Lap-leaper
Tail-swisher
People-carrier.

Lewis White (8)
Two Moors Primary School, Tiverton

Kangaroo

Joey-carrier
Fast-leaper
Tough-boxer
Australian-liver
Green-eater.

Kate Butler (8)
Two Moors Primary School, Tiverton

Penguin Kennings

Ice-skidder
Silly-waddler
White bib-wearer
Fish-eater
Sea-swimmer
Black jacket-wearer
Grey chick-mother
Cold-dweller.

Katie Aldridge (8)
Two Moors Primary School, Tiverton

Cat

Cat-eater
Mouse-hunter
Bird-catcher
Bed-sleeper
Scratch-maker
Tree-climber.

Ryan Hancock (8)
Two Moors Primary School, Tiverton

Cat

Mouse-hunter
Bird-catcher
Tail-twitcher
Fish-taker
Bed-nicker
Miaow-maker.

Georgia Miller (8)
Two Moors Primary School, Tiverton

Puppy

Puddle-maker
Slipper-chewer
Bone-eater
Tail-wagger
Ant-eater
Ball-player
Cat-chaser
Little-barker.

Shannon Jones (8)
Two Moors Primary School, Tiverton

Dog

Meat-eater
Postman-chaser
Slipper-chewer
Tail-wagger
Bone-grabber
Luxury-liver.

Morgan Edgcumbe (8)
Two Moors Primary School, Tiverton

Puppy

Bones-chewer
Puddle-maker
Tail-wagger
Slippers-chewer
Cat-chaser.

Ellie Little (8)
Two Moors Primary School, Tiverton

I See A Penguin

I see a penguin staring at the ice
Its eyes were all beady and small like marbles.
Its skin was all smooth and icy like snow on a hill.
Its beak was like a carrot.
His little feet stuck out like a ballet girl
And last of all its little nails were like tiny spikes.

Rhiannon Clarke (8)
Two Moors Primary School, Tiverton

Puppy

Bird-chaser
Ball-chaser
Bone-chewer
Puddle-maker
Tail-wagger
Bed-nicker.

Daniel Attwood (9)
Two Moors Primary School, Tiverton

Autumn

Sun dies,
Cold comes,
We hide away inside.
Farmers' market comes with food,
Sausages, cheese, all things good.
Across seas, birds migrating,
Black mass in the sky.
Harvest, time for celebration,
Farmers cut crops.
Sun dies,
Cold comes,
We hide away inside.

Tom Parker (11)
Upton Cross Primary School, Nr Liskeard

Autumn Journey

Whirling wind of terror, everybody screams,
Damage and danger everywhere in their midnight dreams.
Twisting and twirling, rumbling and growling
No knowing where it's going
Whirling wind of terror, everybody screams.

Back over the seas and on the sands,
Where school children rush into a building
Like wild fire through a forest
Or a flock of birds joining one another
Gathering together in land.

Then further in we see a farmer
Cut the crops then bale the straw,
Herd the cattle into the barn.
Gathers goods from the garden,
Goes to market to sell and buy,
Sell and buy.

No buyers and it's getting dark,
'Tomorrow,' he mutters, 'tomorrow,
There'll be more because of the conkers,
Leaves and harvest supper,
They'll all be here tomorrow.'

Laura Cottam (10)
Upton Cross Primary School, Nr Liskeard

Crisp Autumn

Birds are migrating across the sea, thundering and grey.
Shops closed, streets dark and ghostly.
Tourists are packing and driving away.
The school bell rings and children run inside.
Farmers get their tractors, drive away to cut the corn.
Crisp autumn is here.

Flapping wings fleeing the land,
To Africa in the sun.
Emptiness flows in the air,
A cold wind blows through the street,
Overloaded cars drive towards the city.
The village is empty.
The teacher flutters with her coffee.
Rain pours down outside.
The field is a crisp brown,
The farmer whistles as he chops,
The sun has travelled to a different country.
The rain has come to do his job.

Hannah-Rose Clay (10)
Upton Cross Primary School, Nr Liskeard

Autumn

The cold weather invades the sunlight, all goes dark today.
The icy evening's killing the flowers as dew lies softly.
Leaves go crispy brown as they get blown away.
Trees bare in the strong wind.
Farmers cut their crops this month, tractors all around.
Giant bales, gallons of corn, tall, fluffy maize to store.
Hurricanes in Florida,
Water - cruel mistress washing down and down.
The rain is heavy, floods wash homes away
Birds fly in fear of cold coming this day
Over frying pan deserts to cool, calming rivers.
The war of light goes on, the clouds take over the day.
Summer's gone, it's all moved on
And the golden, crispy fall has come.

Polly Edwards (10)
Upton Cross Primary School, Nr Liskeard

Best Friends

Jaqueline Wilson,
Your funny and interesting books,
Read, read, read
Just can't stop reading
Bright and exciting.

Best friends,
A cheeky story,
Happy, exciting, gripping
I've read it ten times,
A colourful and fun cover,
Best friends is my very favourite book in the whole world.

Emily Christmas (10)
Wendron CE Primary School, Helston

My Favourite Theme Park

Speeding through the air endlessly
Scraping metal bars
Spookily but fun
Made for family.

Tastes quite sweet
Melts in your mouth
Turns all hard
Fluffy like a sheep.

Bursting out with money
Tickets speeding out,
Beeping for the winner
Flashing orange lights
Using the tickets.

Endless clapping
Nobody cried around here
Daniel laughs and cheers
I had won
No bowing from me
Gentle was the crowd.

Thomas Steggles (10)
Wendron CE Primary School, Helston

Designing A Bookmark On A Computer

Switch it on and ready to go
Ready to have fun, fun, fun
Click on the program
Design a cool bookmark
See it being cut on the machine
Bright coloured acrylic like the sun finished.
Cool!

Lizzy Brookes (10)
Wendron CE Primary School, Helston

Mr Ellis

Mr Ellis said
'Switch on your computers,
We're making bookmarkers,'
Click, click, click
'Find the design sign,
Click on text and type.'
Tap, tap, tap
'When it's finished
E-mail it to them.'
Beep, beep, beep
'Watch the web-cam screen,
Yours is being cut by the laser.'
Zap, zap, zap.
I said
'Hooray, there's mine, it's finished.'
Hip hip hooray, hip hip hooray!

Harriet Wood (10)
Wendron CE Primary School, Helston

Computers

Switch on the computer
There's the icon
Click, click
Hexagon, rectangle, circle which one to pick
Put in the text
Tap, tap
Round the corner
Send the email with instructions
Beep, beep
Arrived at Helston School, great
Linked into the machine
Zap, zap
Look! There's mine,
I made a bookmark!

Rebecca Freeman (10)
Wendron CE Primary School, Helston

Romans

They march into battle
With spears ready to kill
They fire their bows
To kill more men.

They fight in close combat
With swords and shields to kill
They hide some cavalry
To charge in as reinforcements.

Men will die
And men will kill
To win the battle
They'll take risks.

When the battle's won
They'll sail right home
Until another battle's on
Then they'll go again.

Jack Combellack (10)
Wendron CE Primary School, Helston

Primary Design

Wheel up the trolley
Get out my computer
Then turn it on
I can hear it hum,
Up pop the desktops
Click on Primary Design
Choose a shape,
And some writing
Send it to Helston School's cutting machine,
And what comes back
An acrylic bookmark
It is so *fab brilliant super!*

Billy Hartley (10)
Wendron CE Primary School, Helston

. . . ing

Starting,
Running,
Watching,
Learning,
Making,
Choosing,
Designing,
Laughing,
Deleting,
Connecting,
Exciting,
Waiting,
Chatting,
Machining,
Cutting,
Whirring,
Closing,
Finishing,
Tidying,
I designed and made an acrylic bookmark.

Charles Brotherton (10)
Wendron CE Primary School, Helston

Flowers

You're a bunch of violets hiding from the wind,
You're a garden of daffodils waving to each other.
You're a sky of tulips gently blowing back and forth
You're a rose all on your own.
You're a dozen sunflowers dancing in the air.
You're a primrose peeping out in the spring sunshine,
You're a bluebell so small, hanging its bells,
You're flowers that cheer us up!

Lucy White (9)
Wendron CE Primary School, Helston

Computers Are Great

C omputers are ready for us to use
O pen the lid and press the button
M ustn't forget to turn on the program.
P lace a rectangle where you please.
U se the locator to curve the corners
T ap another one inside the first,
E nd with some circles at the top.
R everse and check, delete what's wrong
S o that bit is done all correct.

A re we ready to write the text?
R eally big clear text
E xcellent!

G o to save my work
R eady for the next stage
E mail it in for their cutting machine
A t Helston Community College
T he design's become real!

Helena Fern (9)
Wendron CE Primary School, Helston

Bookmark

Switch on
Where's it gone?
Look for a sign
Then click on 'design'
Which shape shall I use?
Quick, nothing to lose!
Sent to Helston School,
Can't wait. They'll look so cool!
We're watching the machine,
Everyone is so keen,
Got our bookmarks now,
Everyone's shouting, 'Wow!'

Matthew Hawkins (10)
Wendron CE Primary School, Helston

The Feeling

Scoring a goal,
Getting a try,
Winning Wimbledon
        Great feeling.

Hitting a six
Getting the winning punch,
Running down the home straight
        Great feelings.

Winning the Olympics,
Jumping the impossible,
Throwing the impossible
        Great feelings.

Swimming 100m in 52.47,
Running 100m in 9.43,
Winning the 4 x 100m
        Great feelings.

Alex Christmas (8)
Wendron CE Primary School, Helston

My Bookmark

Excited,
Nervous,
Curious,
Ready to start!

Worried,
Hopeful,
Anxious,
It's working!

Delighted,
Happy,
Proud,
Fantastic,
It's finished!

Charlotte Rhodes (9)
Wendron CE Primary School, Helston

I Wish, I Wish

I wish I didn't have homework
I wish I was good at maths
I wish I could have two dogs
I wish I could go to Paris.

I wish I could win a medal
I wish I could have a big pot of gold
I wish I could be a millionaire
I wish I could fly.

I wish I had Legoland all to myself
I wish I could have a quad bike
I wish I could blow up the school
I wish I could have a chicken farm.

I wish I could stay up very late
I wish I could drive a car very fast
I wish I got everything right
I wish I had a good sense of smell.

David Coulston (8)
Wendron CE Primary School, Helston

Colours

Purple is my favourite colour
It's bright and relaxing
Sweet but soft
I like purple.

Red is nice
It's a bush of roses
Sweet smelling and bright
I like red.

Blue is relaxing
Light dark and light
It's a bright sky blue, my school jumper
I like blue.

Alexandra Freeman (9)
Wendron CE Primary School, Helston

Speak To Me

The feel of the wind,
The sound of the morning,
The coldness of the sea,
        Speak to me.

The sound of my dog,
The feeling of my bed,
The heat of the sun,
The taste of cod,
        Speak to me.

The sound of the birds in the morning,
The view of the stars
The blackness of the night,
        Speak to me.

The taste of Chinese,
The feeling of scoring a goal,
The fun of playing with my friends,
        Speak to me.

Jamie Coupland (8)
Wendron CE Primary School, Helston

Horrid Henry

Horrid Henry is so funny
It makes me ache with laughter
Horrid Henry is so funny
When he eats all the honey
Horrid Henry is so funny
When he takes a lot of money
Horrid Henry is so funny
When he spends all his money
Horrid Henry is so funny
When he eats all the sweets
Horrid Henry is so funny
When he sets a stink bomb.

Ross MacNeil (9)
Wendron CE Primary School, Helston

A River

The water is shimmering,
The sound of its trickling
The grass is swaying,
The sun is blazing.

The leaves are diving
The clouds are floating,
The trees are standing,
The bees are buzzing.

The wind is blowing peacefully
The stones are moving rattling and tattling.

The rain starts falling,
The thunder starts crashing,
The lightning starts flashing,
The wind starts howling.

The river starts rising
The storm gets quieter and it's all peaceful again.

Lucy Bray (8)
Wendron CE Primary School, Helston

My Design

Switch on computer
What do I do?
Go onto 'Primary Design'.
What could I do?
Millions of buttons
I think my brain is going to melt
The teacher tells me how to use it
Too many words coming out of his mouth
But I just do it
And now I have my design!

Alexander Hilliard (9)
Wendron CE Primary School, Helston

The Peace Descends

Girls groaning,
Mice squeaking,
Dogs digging,
Cats purring.

Aeroplanes flying,
Water bottles squirting,
Ice cracking,
Sausages sizzling,
Boys reading.

Joseph Posnett (8)
Wendron CE Primary School, Helston

Computer

Clicking, beeping
Looking and drawing
Writing, waiting
Mending and blending
Working, doing
Battery going, going, gone
Forming and destroying
Gone at last.

Thomas Rapson (10)
Wendron CE Primary School, Helston

I Wish I Wish

I wish I had a puppy
I wish I had a kitten
I wish I had a horse
I wish I had a donkey
I wish I had a parrot
I wish I had a budgie.

Louise Jessett (7)
Wendron CE Primary School, Helston

The Garden

Flowers shining,
Grass dancing,
People working,
House creaking,
Children climbing,
Trees blowing
Stones falling
Greenhouse muttering.

Sam Eyres (7)
Wendron CE Primary School, Helston

The Classroom

Children howling,
Whiteboards creaking,
Teachers growling,
Water bottles dripping,
Pictures falling,
Clock stopping,
Computers sleeping,
Door banging,
Windows shutting.

Laura Hesketh (8)
Wendron CE Primary School, Helston

My Bedroom

Floorboards squeaking
Me talking,
Window creaking,
Toys breaking,
Kristin playing,
Shelves wobbling,
Bunk beds standing tall,
Ladder scraping.

Isobel Fern (7)
Wendron CE Primary School, Helston

The Swimming Pool

Splashing water,
Sliding people
Swimming people,
Shouting people,
Screaming children,
Shimmering water,
Shining water,
Damp floor,
Wet towels.

Eleanor Crimmen (8)
Wendron CE Primary School, Helston

The Garden

Children shouting
Bees buzzing
Adults whispering
Swing swinging
Butterflies fluttering
Flowers growing
Snails sliming.

Abigail Beswick Lund (7)
Wendron CE Primary School, Helston

The Beach

Children digging,
Adults bathing,
Kites flying,
Babies paddling,
Boys fishing,
Girls running,
Divers diving,
Lifeguards watching
Sisters screaming.

Jonathan Pascoe (9)
Wendron CE Primary School, Helston

The Park

Parents watching
Children climbing,
Slide shining,
Children concentrating,
Babies quarrelling,
Sun scorching,
Parents groaning,
Swings screeching,
Boys shouting
Girls screaming.

Jake Robertson (8)
Wendron CE Primary School, Helston

I Wish

I wish I had a puppy,
I wish I had earrings,
I wish I could stay up as late as my mum.
I wish my brother would not dress up in my clothes.

Jessica Goodchild (7)
Wendron CE Primary School, Helston

The Beach

Children screaming,
Sun shining,
Adults chatting,
Waves crashing,
Surfers splashing,
Umbrellas flapping,
Sand splatting,
Children playing,
People smiling
Dogs barking,
Seagulls eating.

Rachael Thomas (8)
Wendron CE Primary School, Helston

I Wish

I wish I were an adult
I wish I had straight hair
I wish I had a rabbit,
I wish I could live in Leeds with my nanny.

I wish I had a lot of money,
I wish I could have a cat,
I wish I could win a trophy,
I wish I could beat Kyle.

I wish I were an artist,
I wish I could fly,
I wish I could swim with dolphins.

I wish I could have school dinner everyday
I wish I didn't have freckles,
I wish I had a different name
I wish I could go horse riding.

Claudia Corbridge (8)
Wendron CE Primary School, Helston

The Beach

Children playing
People talking,
Water smashing,
Ice cream stall stelling,
Sand swishing,
Girls and boys eating,
Girls swimming,
Boys surfing,
Waves pushing
Sandcastle building,
Adults sunbathing.
Sun beaming.

Jade Wooderson Harrod (9)
Wendron CE Primary School, Helston

Speak To Me

The beautiful sun that shines,
The horses trotting down the road,
The sound of the calm sea
        Speak to me.

The nice hot relaxing bath,
The way the trees flow in the breeze
The shells on the sandy beach.
        Speak to me.

The beautiful smell of roses
The fun of tree tunnels
The hedgehogs that come into the garden
        Speak to me.

The dolphins that dive up from the sea,
The rains beautiful sound,
The rivers that flow
        Speak to me.

Eloise Thwaites (8)
Wendron CE Primary School, Helston

The Beach

Seagulls squawking,
Waves crashing,
A speedboat zooming,
Children playing,
Dolphins diving,
Sharks snapping,
Dads surfing,
Seaweed swishing,
Fish swimming,
Crabs pinching,
Silence descends.

Joseph Martin (7)
Wendron CE Primary School, Helston

I Wish

I wish I were a sailor
I wish my dad didn't go away,
I wish my parents didn't shout at me.

I wish the teachers didn't shout at me
I wish my sister played with me
I wish the work was not so hard like it is.

I wish I were rich
I wish nobody got hurt
I wish there was no such thing as school
I wish I were you.

Nicholas Phillips (7)
Wendron CE Primary School, Helston

I Wish

I wish I had a dog,
I wish my hair was straight,
I wish school was cool.

I wish I had a pony so I could ride it,
I wish I could have a house
I wish I could have a bike.

Amber Wooderson Harrod (7)
Wendron CE Primary School, Helston

I Wish

I wish I had long nails
I wish I had long eyelashes
I wish I had nice lips
I wish I had red cheeks
I wish I got to stay up late
I wish I had lots of ice cream.

Emily Rhodes (7)
Wendron CE Primary School, Helston

I Wish

I wish I had security
I wish I had super powers
I wish I was in Lord of the Rings
I wish I was speedy.

I wish I was still in Class Two
I wish I was a knight
I wish I was older then the queen
I wish girls weren't so bossy.

I wish I could stay at home
I wish!

William Jose (7)
Wendron CE Primary School, Helston

Stormy Night

Thunder crashing,
Lightning flashing,
People screaming,
Cars crashing,
Rain pouring,
Trees falling,
People dying.

Niamh Cook (8)
Wendron CE Primary School, Helston

I Wish

I wish I could talk to animals
I wish I was a vet
I wish I was a robin
I wish I could swim in the sea
I wish I was an artist
I wish I could stay up late.

Lowena Mudge (7)
Wendron CE Primary School, Helston

Speak To Me

The smell of flowers,
The heat of fire,
The fun of school,
The messiness of art,
    Speak to me.

The fun of toys,
The sound of children playing,
The noise of ketchup,
The sound of birds,
    Speak to me.

The brightness of the sun,
The quiet of the classroom,
The noise of the TV,
The night with the red Indians
    Speak to me.

The best of the CDs
The funniness of my granny
The fun of surfing,
The sound of the wind,
    They all speak to me.

Alice Harry (8)
Wendron CE Primary School, Helston

The Beach

Waves bouncing
Children splashing,
Crabs snapping
People eating,
Children finding,
Children jumping,
Grown-ups sleeping
Children catching,
What a crazy beach!

Gabrielle Slater (7)
Wendron CE Primary School, Helston

I Wish

I wish I had a pet mouse
I wish I could have ten pounds a day
I wish I were rich
I wish I could run away to London.

I wish I was good
I wish I had a puppy
I wish I had a TV of my own
I wish I could go to the moon.

I wish I could have sweets everyday
I wish I could be 3 again.
I wish I were queen
I wish I had a horse.

Heather MacNeil (7)
Wendron CE Primary School, Helston

My Mum

My mum is my mum
She is so fun
She makes me laugh
And loves me so.

And when I cry
She holds me tight
And I see the night
The starry night
And she holds me
All through that starry night.

My mum is my mum
She is so fun
She makes me laugh
And loves me so.

Holly Hobbs (10)
Widewell Primary School, Plymouth

X Fear Factor

Darkness all around me
Shadows all I see
My heart is thumping
I hear noises bumping
Fear is all I feel
But ghosts and ghouls aren't real
So under my covers I will lay
Until the morning light of day.

Dylan Gowlett (9)
Widewell Primary School, Plymouth

My Poem

In comes a skeleton
In comes a ghost
In comes a monster
Munching toast.

Go away skeleton
Go away ghost
Go away monster
Munching toast.

George Harding (9)
Widewell Primary School, Plymouth

Winter

Snow falls gently on the ground,
A cold chilling breeze all around,
The trees are leafless and bare,
The sound of Christmas in the air,
Snowball fights lasting till the night,
Put your hat and scarf on
And listen to the carol singers burst into song.

Loren Smith (9)
Widewell Primary School, Plymouth

Love Poem

I am so grateful,
I am in love,
It's as white,
As white as a dove.

It sounds like a harmony,
Singing so loud,
Although you can hear it,
It makes you feel proud.

It feels so great,
As it touches my heart,
I always know
That he is a part.

I am so grateful
I am in love,
It's as white
As white as a dove.

Katie Fallick (11)
Widewell Primary School, Plymouth

Robin Hood

For the good of all the men,
And the love of just one woman
He fought to uphold the justice
By breaking the city's law
Through stormy days
And winter's nights
Cold, wet, hungry and tired
He stole from the rich
And gave to the poor
With an army of peasants by his side
Marion, Little John and everyone else
Fighting for justice
By breaking the law.

Frances Bennison-Reseigh (10)
Widewell Primary School, Plymouth

Mental Maths

Mental maths
Isn't bad
I just love it
I'm not mad.

Solving sums
I do enjoy
To work them out
I use a ploy.

I think so hard
And use my brain
I think of a problem
Again and again.

The solution pops
Into my head
And at the end
I go to bed.

But if I'm stumped
It's not so bad,
'Cause then it's simple
I ask my dad.

Andrew Hunter (10)
Widewell Primary School, Plymouth

Winter

The trees are bare
Like the cold winter air
The children are freezing cold.

They wear the hats and scarves
As the cold wind blows.

The families go out for bonfire night
And buy some food and drink
Their friends come along as the cold wind blows.

Shannon Limbrick (10)
Widewell Primary School, Plymouth

My Dad

My dad is so fun,
He loves me as much as my mum,
My dad makes me laugh when I'm in the bath.
And when I go to bed he tickles me like Fred,
He loves to play with me when I'm so lonely,
He takes me to lots of places
That's why my dad is so fun.

Connor Palfreeman (10)
Widewell Primary School, Plymouth

What Do You Want?

What do you want?
I want a dinosaur
I like a dinosaur
I need a dinosaur
Vicious and terrifying
Huge and petrifying
Living in a lost world.

Give me
A triceratops
Give me
A stegasauras
Give me
A bracasaurus.

Make it real
Make it see
Like its really mine
I only want a dinosaur.

Max Lewin (9)
Withycombe Raleigh CE School, Exmouth

The Seasons

The seasons are a special thing
Summer, winter, autumn and spring
They're the things that bring
The sun, the snow, the leaves, the frost
Without the seasons we'd be lost.

Spring comes first, it brings newborns
Brings new life to things old and worn
Flowers spring from the ground
The birds make their beautiful sound
Spring is a nice season all around.

Summer is next in line
Summer is a favourite of mine
It's that lovely hot time
The sun in its place in the sky
If anyone didn't like summer
I'd wonder why.

Now its autumn the leaves start to die
The leaves on the ground
The sun in the sky
Conkers are falling
Winter is calling
We're almost in the month
Where frost spreads on the ground.

Here we are, winter at last
The snow and the ice is spreading fast
Darker days and longer nights
Ice skating and snowball fights
The winter coldness gripping the earth
But sadly winter has to disappear
And spring takes the job to pass on throughout the year.

Ben Mellish (9)
Withycombe Raleigh CE School, Exmouth

My Rats

My rats are
Run out of the cage
Sort of rats.

They are
Take me out
Help me out
Kind of rats.

They are
Eat a lot
Drink a lot
Smell a lot
Kind of rats.

They are
All mine.

Max Williams (9)
Withycombe Raleigh CE School, Exmouth

Autumn Hints

Arms and legs in the cold sun,
Noses like ice lollies on a frozen stick.
Unlucky shadows warming on a field
As children stand on the edge and stare.
Travellers passing through the undergrowth in darkness,
Unexpected animals hibernating in the dark.
Misty days of October after the darkness of night.

Jack Greenhalgh (9)
Withycombe Raleigh CE School, Exmouth

My Black Cat

My black cat she stretches out
Like a panther in the sun
Warming her whiskers, she sharpens her claws
Stretching her paws
To the furniture.

She lies so still
In her permanent pit
On the settee.

Sometimes she likes to play
Chasing her ball
Up and down in the hall,
My black cat.

Chris Rundle (9)
Withycombe Raleigh CE School, Exmouth

Mrs Wigglebottom

She eats like a pig,
Her wig is black,
Her lips are sacks
And has a lot of racks,
Where her tummy should be.
Mrs Wigglebottom
She never wears cotton,
So she moans and she groans
And destroys all she owns
She has such big bones
Under her flabby skin.

Lianna Webber (9)
Withycombe Raleigh CE School, Exmouth

My Dad

My dad is
A get on your bike kind of dad
My dad.

My dad is
A make a train or a plane kind of dad
My dad.

My dad is
A go to the beach kind of dad
My dad.

My dad is
A have some fun kind of dad
My dad.

Andrew Burrow (9)
Withycombe Raleigh CE School, Exmouth

I Wish

I wish kids could stay up late
I wish I could rule the whole state.
I wish there was no such thing as school.
I wish every house had a swimming pool.
I wish I had a chocolate bar,
I wish I was a pop star.
I wish I was as small as a mouse.
I wish that I had my own house.
I wish I had a big red balloon,
I wish I could travel to the moon
So many wishes I can see,
Have you as many wishes as me?

Mia Weeks (9)
Withycombe Raleigh CE School, Exmouth

Autumn Touch On The School Field

Outside in the autumn air.
The rooks glide without a care.
Leaves still hang from treetops high.
And the sun is rising in the sky.
An artist's paint is flicked on the trees.
And fields are like a million seas.

The animals are running around.
Their little feet go pound, pound, pound.
It is beautiful, this silent time
And killing it is like a crime.
But children will come out to play
And with their shouts
Chase it away.

Jimmy Wangdi (9)
Withycombe Raleigh CE School, Exmouth

A Hint Of Autumn

Autumn is a time of season
When leaves fall,
And diamonds sit in the grass
Made to glisten by the sun.
Squirrels go racing by
Carrying treasure for winter,
Like naughty robbers,
They steal food put out for birds.
Autumn is a lovely time,
Making a promise of Christmas.

Ryan Neville (9)
Withycombe Raleigh CE School, Exmouth